Table of Contents

PHILOSOPHICAL PERSPECTIVES

Jochen Kirchhoff

Living Cosmology Essays

on the World Crisis

PHILOSOPHICAL PERSPECTIVES

Jochen Kirchhoff

Living Cosmology Essays

on the World Crisis

edition *dionysos*

Bibliographic information of the German National Library:
The German National Library lists this publication in the German National Bibliography; detailed bibliographic data is available on the Internet at http://dnb.dnb.de.

Author: Jochen Kirchhoff
Translation: Wolfram Bahmann, Amélie de Branges
Layout & typesetting: Wolfram Bahmann, Uli Fischer
Cover photo: pixabay
Publisher: BoD - Books on Demand GmbH
                        In de Tarpen 42, 22848 Norderstedt
                        bod@bod.de
Printing: Libri Plureos GmbH
                        Friedensallee 273, 22763 Hamburg
ISBN: 978-3-7693-8900-5

Foreword

The world crisis is keeping us in suspense. It did not begin yesterday, and it is not going to be over tomorrow either. It reaches into the deepest layers of human consciousness and the cosmos and affects all our lives directly and every day, and not only in the abysmal geopolitical intrigues and their reflections in the crises of German society.

No other author has devoted himself to overcoming the world crisis with such philosophical depth and breadth as Jochen Kirchhoff. No other author focuses so much on the deep forces of being human and their potential to bring about a comprehensive transformation of conditions in the cosmic context.

The essays collected here reflect his impulses in the "struggles of the time" of the Corona crisis as well as timeless themes of human existence in the mirror of the seasons and his tireless criticism of the natural sciences that dominate human consciousness.

Eleven essays were published in the online magazine manova.news, one in the Cicero online magazine and another on the website of the Institute for Critical Social Research. For the kind permission to use the texts for print publication, many thanks to the editors responsible, Roland Rottenfußer, Michael Meyen and Ralf Hanselle.

The continuity of our collaboration with Manova is particularly appreciated – the essays republished here stand side by side with a wealth of political and social analysis, as well as spiritual inspiration and encouraging texts on mental self-help, which in their intensity and truthfulness have become an indispensable alternative force in the media landscape.

May these essays by Jochen Kirchhoff, in their peculiar style, which was, so to speak, wrested from the medium of the Internet and its writing requirements, reach their readers in their rebirth as readable paperback texts in the spirit of Kirchhoff's thoughts:

> *You, as a human, are meant by the universe.*
> *You can make the difference and live up to your*
> *dignity as a spiritual-cosmic being by*
> *recognising, accepting and creatively perceiving*
> *yourself as an integral part of the whole.*
> *It's about time. –*

Uli Fischer and Wolfram Bahmann
in December 2024

Philosophy
and
Contemporary History

"At What Point Do We Stand?"

Giorgio Agamben

The Corona Blues

For the time being, the coronavirus crisis has passed without a sound bite. Only a minority would like to seriously touch it. So sponge over it. Or should we? Just no reappraisal that could open up old wounds and remind the followers and yes-men of their own blindness and cowardice. That seems to be the majority consensus for now. There are other voices, but they don't get through.

But feeling morally superior now because you "knew it back then" is of little use. My point here is different. I want to outline some of my impressions of the last three years, to which I also attribute representative character, and draw conclusions from them.

When the corona craze started, I felt caught off guard, so it took me a while to sort out the terrain and begin to realise what was actually happening here. What is this? Who is directing here? What is the substance of it? How am I supposed to deal with this, both personally and publicly? What is rolling towards us? It quickly became clear that it wasn't about health. But then what was it about? Was it the super-rich, the big corporations, the pharmaceutical industry, manipulated and bought politicians, malicious and greedy powers that cleverly launched and controlled the crisis in order to ruin and subjugate us? Questions of this kind arose and I tried to face them.

I have to say here that at the beginning of 2020, my thinking as a philosopher was primarily apolitical. For a long time, I had a strong defence against anything political. And this was based on a deep mistrust. The student movement, which I witnessed at the Free University in Berlin, didn't politicise me in the usual sense of the word at the age of 23/24. I somehow stayed on the outside, watching the whole thing without being deeply affected by it. It was different when the Wall came down and reunification happened. It gripped me immediately, challenged me and mobilised energies for action in me that I had hardly known before. I wanted to influence, shape and participate in a broad sense.

This was certainly reinforced by my friendship with Rudolf Bahro, the well-known GDR dissident, who was deported to the West at the end of the 1970s and now also became politically active here, motivated in a broad ecological sense, driven by the basic impulse to use the ecological crisis to bring about a complete reorganisation of society, which also had spiritual traits. At the time, I thought this was the right approach in the first reading and in the basic line, despite objections in detail and also in principle. We talked and discussed it a lot. I started teaching at Humboldt University in the autumn of 1990. Initially social ecology, then increasingly natural philosophy and criticism of science. At some point my political vigour died out. I returned to philosophy.

It wasn't until Corona that I became fundamentally politicised again, so to speak. It was clear to me that now, in or from spring 2020, it was a matter of clearly showing my colours, understanding what was actually going on here and drawing very concrete conclusions that would be reflected in action, which is what happened. And this naturally took place in the context of my philosophical activities and research. As a philosopher, I felt I had a duty, so to speak. Increasingly, the impulse grew in me to mentally penetrate the increasingly massive, threatening and also grotesque corona spectacle with a cool head and to raise my voice without direct political actionism, which I considered to be misguided.

The absurd figures in the computer models used to quickly make policy showed me that those in power were orientating themselves to the prevailing abstract natural science, and that they were doing so with a dizzying lack of awareness of the deeper connections between this approach to the world. The general public accepted everything humbly. That didn't surprise me.

The kowtowing – not only by intellectuals – to the natural sciences and mathematics had been familiar to me for many years. The only thing that was astonishing and new to me was the fact that this affinity for science was now being translated one-to-one into political action and determining the fate of millions of people.

All the errors and mistakes of abstract natural science were adopted without a hint of critical reflection. The epistemological assumptions of the abstract model calculations and predictions presented everywhere were initially not critically analysed at all and then only very occasionally. They proved to be consistently wrong. Nothing was true that was loudly claimed and propagated and on which the political corona measures were based.

Most of the so-called intellectuals, who piously and devotedly accepted every delusion from this direction as if it had to be that way, were completely lacking in this respect. I found it an unworthy and embarrassing spectacle. Most of them were not at all responsive to this point and dismissed everything. The majority of them trusted what they believed to be science or what was presented to them as having no alternative. And here I don't just mean the political appropriation of science, i. e. its manipulation in the service of the powerful – that was evident enough – but this science itself as an abstract principle of knowledge, which in its basic approach excluded life and consciousness and thus cemented the idea or illusion of a dead and meaningless universe.

The first lockdown in Germany – to use this dubious term from the penal system – from 22 March 2020 had a spooky effect on me. From my flat, you can see a playground that was always full of life. Now there was a paralysing silence. No more children's laughter. The whole area was cordoned off like a restricted military zone. Incidentally, as many will remember, the skies were clear for weeks at a time. An unimaginable and magical clarity. A stark contrast to the collective madness that had increasingly gripped society. And this madness, as it then turned out, gained supremacy not only in Germany, but in many countries.

My nights became increasingly difficult. I often lay awake for long periods, brooding over the nightmarish events that now seemed to dominate everything. Corona in the morning, corona in the evening. Corona as a constant topic. The media went into overdrive. The collective fear of the virus was palpable. People staggered blindly into a horror film staged by those in power. The mask became a religious symbol. Those who refused to wear it were increasingly in trouble. The police made themselves the beacons of the ruling politicians and in many places acted with unprecedented brutality and dullness.

The fear of a killer virus that would soon kill millions of people, the fear of being infected by this tiny monster and of fellow human beings as virus carriers and virus spreaders, was joined by the fear of the brutally blind state power.

Arguments of a critical nature that emerged here and there, especially in the alternative media, were not echoed by the aligned public, but met with fierce resistance. I noted in my diary on 8 March 2020: "The front is closing in."

Over and over again, for weeks on end, this clear sky, this light of cosmic majesty, a sky that arched over a society dominated by fear and delusion, as if a demon had set out to whip us all into destruction, into annihilation. Or what was it? Who was painfully interfering with us? And this on a planetary scale. I felt it to be a campaign against the genuinely human and living in favour of demonic and killing principles. Why, I pondered, do people allow this to happen to them? Because they accept it, believe it to be right, or because they are forced to do so, regardless of how they feel about it?

I increasingly realised that my fear of the virus had become a primal fear of death itself. Corona was death itself. Corona was the Grim Reaper. This fiction had countless people in its grip. When I was sitting on the S-Bahn (suburban railway) in autumn 2020, as so often without a mask, a woman called out to me as she left the train: "Have fun in intensive care!"

At some point, there was only one relevant death, the one caused by Covid. All other deaths hardly counted. The corona-viruses, which had actually been known for many years, became all-dominating and treacherous monsters. The famous PCR test conjured them up again and again. The positively tested was now considered contaminated and therefore ill. And everything had to be done to protect the community from him. Anyone could be the unconscious murderer of the other. Therefore: masks on, everywhere if possible.

A transcendental religion of masks, faith in the state and an unbridled fetishism of measures emerged. The unmasked and thus unruly contemporary was the egotistical and anti-social pest that any fool could, indeed should, rudely take to task. I felt like I was in an open psychiatric ward. Or like in an open-air prison. "In the wrong film" anyway.

As far as masks were concerned, I had observed early on that many people wore them with a certain fervour, like members of a sect, and that they were perceived as conveying significance. Finally, life had a purpose that you could orientate yourself towards, that you could feel, that impressed itself on your face and made breathing difficult, which was occasionally uncomfortable even for mask fans. But: the suffering was obviously part of it. I wear a mask, therefore I am. I suffer, but I help others, I serve humanity. I am in solidarity. To do this, I have to hide my face and therefore my individuality. You are nothing, corona is everything, must be everything, because that's the only way we can succeed and defeat the virus monster.

Behind or under the mask, as I often observed, there was a ticking fear, a panicked fear of infection with all its consequences. Since people were tirelessly persuaded of this, it cannot be condemned per se. The panic was created shamelessly and perfidiously. The fear machine ran almost non-stop.

Then there was the political pressure. The state took brutal action wherever there was resistance to the measures. Many people effectively mutated into corona police officers who issued rude and harsh orders. I experienced that time and time again.

I asked myself, with the Italian philosopher Giorgio Agamben: "At What Point Do We Stand?" (This was the title of an essay by Agamben from 20 March 2020.) At the latest when I understood that the prevailing narrative of the killer virus and the need for massive restrictions by means of drastic measures was apparently accepted and supported by the majority of people and that rational arguments against it had almost zero effect, I realised many things and my attention sharpened. I noticed that the grotesque and the banal were winning out across the board , making their presence felt pompously, and that everything seemed to be designed to turn Germany into a cultural and intellectual desert in which masked sectarians were in charge, posing as saviours and philanthropists.

The official lies became ever more stupid and massive.

Although more and more pillars of the ruling madness collapsed in being dismantled by clever minds – such as the PCR test or the absurd incidences – this initially had hardly any major impact. For a long time, people tested like the devil.

Then came the next step: the propagation and introduction of so-called vaccination. There was the threat of compulsory vaccination. Like other unvaccinated people, I wondered how I should behave if I was confronted with brutal coercion to be vaccinated. I explored the most diverse options. None seemed to me to be beyond any doubt. Then the vaccination requirement was dropped.

As an unvaccinated person and non-car driver, I found it difficult to leave the confines of my home during the so-called 2G regulations (vaccinated or recovered) – I wasn't allowed to use public transport. Of course, I did it anyway. Wherever possible, without a mask. Occasionally, the mask was necessary so as not to give the corona gangs any reason to check me and, if necessary, ask me to leave the train. I got through almost everywhere, which I found somehow amazing. With a normal ticket, but without a passenger permit. In an emergency, I took a taxi. Or I could get people close to me to transport me to my destination. As most people are drivers, they often didn't even think about my situation. I was almost embarrassed to point this out.

I found the vaccination campaign particularly disgusting and humiliating. The devastating damage caused by this so-called vaccination also increasingly came to light. It still remains a sensitive and largely taboo area, as we know.

Corona blues. Rather a mild formula when you think of this nightmare that still somehow surrounds us poisoning the atmosphere like toxic. air. The many corona lies have still not been fully exposed. The collective silence, especially about so-called vaccinations, is insidious and poisonous. I sometimes wish there was some kind of world tribunal. And that doesn't just apply to corona-virus. It basically applies to all the murderous madness on this maltreated planet. Corona is just one of the latest manifestations of this madness.

I often stood at the sub-urban train station and struggled to realise that I was deprived of the simple freedom to get on the next train.

I saw people getting on and off the bus and wondered whether they realised that they now had a kind of privilege that had been taken away from me and many other unvaccinated people. I suspect that most of them didn't care at all.

And that was the scary thing. It wasn't tragic, rather eerily trivial. You could take it a few steps further. And I did that occasionally. Where would the spook end? How far would the rulers go?

The corona madness initially seemed like a break with civilisation, but when viewed in the light of day, it was "only" the logical continuation and intensification of trends that had been underway for a long time. It was already clear beforehand that the cultural and civilisational values so often invoked would not be able to withstand a real endurance test.

Decades ago, I already thought the varnish of the bourgeois world was very thin. Just a slight twist and it would shatter.

And that, I thought, would unleash devastatingly destructive energies. At the latest since the hell of the First World War, every attentive observer of historical events should have been aware of this.

And yet still: corona was a turning point that can hardly be overestimated, a blow, so to speak, that shattered many things and brought to light what had been considered impossible. Fundamental social agreements were abruptly overturned. And with astonishing speed ...

What I believe I have understood about the corona-virus crisis can be summarised as follows: even reasonably peaceful and compatible contemporaries can quickly become a mob that brutally and fanatically defames, denigrates and marginalises and, where it is deemed necessary, also strikes when rebellious subjects stand in its way. Falling to a quasi-archaic level of consciousness, where people act out of the pack, remains a possibility for the majority of people. "But if

I don't like something, my principle is to get rid of it", as Wilhelm Busch says.

You can persuade people of almost anything and make it plausible, even if it is absurd, as long as it is sufficiently convincing in the way presented by government and scientific authorities. That sounds cynical, but it cannot be seriously disputed. Thinking for yourself is a rarity.

Reason counts for little in the crisis. Science is held up like a monstrance by those in power, while quasi-religious dogmas dominate the field, sanctioned by a yes-man morality that tolerates no deviations.

What does it do to a thoughtful and sensitive person realizing that he or she is living in a delusional system that most people around believe to be reality?

State terrorism, as practised by the corona regimes, is generally based on a deficient image of humanity; people are degraded to mere bodies and robbed of their metaphysical substance, in which their human dignity is ultimately rooted. At the same time, anything spiritual or considered "esoteric" is denigrated and politically categorised as belonging to the "right-wing spectrum".

There will be no return to the pre-corona state. Corona has exposed frightening mentalities, including the desire of those in power to authoritarianise their actions and the apathy of the masses.

The many new and lively contacts that I made in the "dissident scene" during the corona-virus years were very pleasing for me; I met alert and critical people here that I would never have met without the corona-virus. There was something encouraging about that. It never resulted in a kind of forced consensus.

I've often asked myself that, even before corona. I still believe in an indestructible creative potential in people, even if this is usually rather buried. At some point, the darkness could – and will – lift. However, without the spiritual-cosmic factor, to put it this way, it will not work. The question of the human-cosmos relation, which has determined and driven my thinking for more than half a century, demands an answer. Abstract natural science cannot provide this answer, nor can religions. I am struggling to find this answer.

The first step, I believe, will and must be to recognise that we live in an all around living world and that a "you-are-not-meant-universe" of monstrous emptiness and meaninglessness is an illusion that is ruining us.

* * *

Torn between East and West

In the West, Rudolf Bahro co-founded the Green Party, which he soon left because he recognised it as a "system party". But I don't want to talk about that. I had been friends with Bahro since the summer of 1988. When he was in West Berlin for a few days in the autumn of that year, he stayed with me. Our breakfast conversations were almost endless. We "philosophised" without restraint, so to speak, thinking about how we could "stir up" Germany. It went very far. Perhaps too far. Beethoven played a certain role in this; we were both ardent admirers of the man and his music. We talked about him again and again in the course of our friendship. Listening to a Beethoven string quartet with Bahro was an experience in itself. I have met few people who could listen to classical music with such intensity and concentration as he did.

I had contacted Bahro in the spring of 1988 because I was impressed by his book "Logik der Rettung (Logic of Salvation)". I didn't agree with everything, but that was of secondary importance. The book was a great, in parts certainly naïve draft, but I thought it had enormous appeal. Many people criticised the book at the time. Some critics even ridiculed it. I found that to be rather unfair and ignorant.

So-called reunification was initially out of the question. Bahro didn't want it anyway. When it came, he was against it. He lived in Niederstadtfeld in the Eifel (low mountain range) region, far away from Berlin. There he was the central figure of a small ecological-spiritual community. In the "green environment", he was often treated as a kind of curiosity. Beethoven, Hölderlin, Hegel, Meister Eckhart, Luther, Müntzer and many others of this calibre were, so to speak, comrades-in-arms for Bahro, whom he often and gladly invoked. For him, they were not primarily historical figures, but living contemporaries. Hardly anyone could or wanted to go along with that. I could, even though our comrades in arms were not always identical. Beethoven certainly was. We couldn't do without Beethoven. As far as Müntzer was concerned, he seemed to think he was a reincarnation of him. In any case, there were always statements that pointed in this direction.

"..die nicht mit den Wölfen heulen (..Who Doesn't Howl With the Wolves)" is the title of a volume of essays by Bahro (written between 1967 and 1969), which is primarily about Beethoven, and secondarily about Hölderlin and Fichte. At the end, Beethoven's late works are explored, especially the last quartets. In the Great Fugue, he writes, there is "no behaviour, not a single ritardando, no crescendo, no decrescendo, despite the threatening sharpness of the situation. The hero sticks to his march with fascinating persistence. Whoever is able to stride out like this has been prepared for everything before he has taken the first step". Bahro's idealistic self-stylisation also resonated here, breaking through again and again. Mostly indirectly, occasionally directly. Critics said: He overestimates himself excessively.

Although Bahro liked to describe himself as a "product of the GDR", his actual roots were deeper, as the reference to the aforementioned comrades-in-arms indicates. He saw himself as an exemplary German, so to speak, without ever using such a formulation.
He was interested in the Germans and pondered what they

were all about. The Germans, Nietzsche once said, "are from the day before yesterday and the day after tomorrow".

This could easily be applied to Bahro as well. Bahro and I, together with Rainer Langhans, once led a seminar which, as I recall, had the succinct and also abysmal title: "What is German?". My book "Nietzsche, Hitler and the Germans", for which Bahro had written a foreword and which was published shortly after the fall of the Berlin Wall, also played a part in this. I rather doubt whether we got any closer to the "German enigma" in that seminar. I don't remember whether there was a recording. It would be possible. But such recordings were rather rare back then.

Bahro and I talked about the GDR (German Democratic Republic) again and again. He could never completely detach himself from this topic, which was quite understandable. I learnt a lot from him about the history of the GDR. For Bahro, the SED (socialist united party) as a party was a religion. When I once, in return, labelled the ruling ideology of this party as materialism, Bahro spoke against it with a vehemence that irritated me. In his famous speech at the extraordinary party conference of the still-SED on 16 December 1989, which then led to the renaming of the SED, this was clearly noticeable. Bahro spoke out of a deep emotional concern. Many delegates responded to his words with scorn and derision. For example, when he spoke of the "all-German car society" that was now dawning.

Bahro gave me the notes to his speech beforehand. One day after the party conference, he visited me and told me, agitated and upset, what had happened. I had never seen him so affected before. It was clearly about politics and religion. With Bahro, it always was. The one could never be separated from the other.

Rudolf Bahro never relegated the GDR to the scrapheap of history. He also stood by his former party career in the SED. He had not the slightest intention of distancing himself from his GDR past as a party functionary in the familiar and embarrassing manner. He even offered the imprisoned Honecker to testify on his behalf in court – which he refused – knowing full well that it was Honecker who had given him an eight-year prison sentence.

He never looked at his Stasi (state security agency) file. It didn't interest him at all. That impressed me. You can also find it strange. It certainly had something to do with his enormous self-confidence. He would have considered it beneath his dignity to join the "victor's justice" practised everywhere by the West.

Incidentally, I took the term "victor's justice" in this context from Bahro.

Somehow Bahro was unique, hardly comparable with other dissidents. He came from far away. And that sustained him. It gave him stability. Ultimately, it was history that he saw himself as a part of and co-creator of. The postmodern nihilism of "anything goes" was alien to him. He countered it, if you want to call it that, with a metaphysical impulse of will, although he tended to avoid the word metaphysics.

Rudolf Bahro died on 5 December 1997 and was buried in the cemetery Dorotheenstädtischer Friedhof. I gave the eulogy on 12 December. Towards the end of the speech it says:

"Who was Rudolf Bahro, what was Rudolf Bahro? I have often thought about this and I have not found a completely satisfactory answer. Perhaps he was a mystically orientated politician or a politically orientated mystic, a monk who felt the urge to be a cultural revolutionary, half Luther, half Müntzer, a reformer – when he handed me his 'Alternative' in the summer of 1988, he wrote inside: 'For Jochen Kirchhoff, my utopia of the Russian Revolution' – a reformer of a church that then dissolved into nothingness. Perhaps he was – and sometimes I had this suspicion – a musician who lacked the opportunity to live out his talents. He was a thinker who didn't really want to think, but to work and act. Like many thinkers, especially German thinkers, he longed for the great, liberating deed. Then again, he was a spiritual, meditative man."

Rudolf Bahro has been largely forgotten. Hardly anyone refers to him in a positive way. This will not change for the time being. The zeitgeist is blowing in a completely different direction. He would be – and he was – a disruptive factor. More than most people think. But being a disruptive factor today is not a shortcoming, but rather an honour. Assuming, of course, that this disruption is of a productive and intelligent nature, not a dull and unreflective rebellion of the kind we are all too familiar with.

Anyone who engages with Bahro, and this can be quite controversial, will come across a number of ideas that are worth exploring. You don't have to agree with him all around. But one can certainly have respect for the seriousness of his "spiritual and moral will". In the field of tension between East and West, he was a representative figure who is worth remembering. At least that's what I think. Otherwise I wouldn't have written this little text, which has turned into a kind of Bahro homage. But perhaps that's not a mistake ...

* * *

Philosophy
and
Rhythm of Life

"Now everything,

everything must change"

Ludwig Uhland

The Return of Life

Time and again, I have had the impression that spring is both a challenge and an excessive demand for many people in the western world. That sounds strange, perhaps disconcerting. What is it about?

First of all, it should be noted that although so-called modern man is occasionally moved by the sublimity and beauty of nature, and indeed seeks it out in order to escape everyday life, he cannot – and usually does not want to – really break out of the corset of his rationality and sobriety, and in this respect he is more or less safe from overly strong, possibly deeply moving, even overwhelming impressions.

If you really face up to what happens in spring, if you take in deeply the bursting forth, sprouting manifestation in overwhelming abundance and splendour that can be observed everywhere, not only marvelling and delighting, but also let yourself be touched spiritually and emotionally, a transformation takes place.

Why? Because growth and becoming per se are manifesting, forming shape, out of the invisible into the visible. Origin and shape: a great and deep connection that cannot be fathomed or contemplated to the end.

Many people are embarrassed by this. They fear making a fool of themselves or slipping into sentimental kitsch if they openly declare that their soul is expanding, drunk on beauty as it were. Incidentally, wherever the splendour of spring flowers is used in advertising, for example for a cosmetic product or a holiday destination, it is often mercilessly appealing to precisely this emotional kitsch, in the knowledge that it can be easily and quickly recalled.

In our latitudes, spring is always the great transformer and bringer forth, which suddenly and as if by magic breaks open everything that is frozen and hidden in winter, manifesting it into overwhelming visibility, bringing the dormant and pupated into the dazzling fullness of light. Forms emerge from the quasi-nothing, increasingly lush and numerous, if you let them and don't smother them in the noise and dust of urban wasteland and misuse them as a fashionable and quickly consumable patchwork.

"Now everything, everything must change", says a poem by Ludwig Uhland, which Schubert set to music in a haunting way.

> "The world grows more beautiful with each passing day,
> We don't know what else may come,
> The blossoming will not end."

These are the lines of the text. A kind of utopia is revealed, a promise that always has to do with hope. With hope for the turning point, the great, liberating turning point that connects us to the light and shows us ways out of the wasteland, out of the violence and the deeply gnawing feeling of meaninglessness.

Spring, the beauty of nature in general, has a meaningful effect, and if not that, then it is uplifting and encouraging. Perhaps there is meaning behind and in everything after all. Perhaps not everything is in vain after all. Perhaps we are not lost after all. Perhaps the madness we produce or tolerate is not the last word after all.

Everything, everything could change. And this is signalled by the events of spring. It resonates with us, even if it is often disregarded or devalued as deceptive and false. Beauty is then suspected of being a lie, even if this actually seems absurd.

What delights people about spring is not only what it shows in a sensually enchanting way, but also what it proclaims beyond all that. That the darkness will be overcome and the light will triumph. That everything can and will change – which has already been hinted at – that the air is full of promise, the promise of another, deeper spring.

I am not afraid to speak of the metaphysical dimension of spring. Spring proves, fundamentally so to speak, that creative potential, even as a great change, is not a phantasmagoria, but a reality. That solidified things can be dissolved. That we are integrated into a great cycle that brings us back to the light. Light triumphs, abundance triumphs, beauty triumphs. These victories make us happy and help us. Everything becomes lighter, more permeable, more open. The beginning itself becomes tangible. That is it too.

Of course, spring in the mountains is different to spring in the flat north. And: there is a more southern and a more northern spring. It seems almost trivial to point this out, but it's not. Spring is never trivial, irrelevant or boring. For in it a powerful arc is spanned. In this respect, there is great tension in the air. A great, mysterious movement towards the other, the higher, the further ...

In Italian, spring is called Primavera. Think of the famous painting by Botticelli. Perhaps it means something like "the first true thing"? Is that it? Is beauty true? What does it proclaim? Is this beauty good? These questions are based on the Neoplatonic equation of the good with the beautiful and the

true, which has been argued over for centuries. Is this equation not "somehow" anchored in us, regardless of what scientists and intellectuals and sceptics of all stripes say about it? I would like to ponder this.
The spring of May 1945 is said to have been particularly impressive and beautiful.

The laying down of arms after years of murderous war coincided with this spring's splendour. Shocking and emotionally almost unbearable, as can be seen from many testimonies. Spring and peace. Hölderlin's great poem "Peace Celebration" shines through. What do we do with it, beyond sentimentality, kitsch and phoney feelings?

Spring is and remains a major challenge. Will we pass it?

* * *

Fullness of Light of the Living

Summer sings its very own song when it fulfils what is associated with it in the majority of our latitudes and has become a place of longing: the warmth, the abundance of light and the wealth of colours and shapes that reach over from spring and then increasingly disappear. This very special song also embraces me, the person born at the height of summer as it sings to me, stimulates my singing. Calming me, revitalising me, letting me be. Or grants me beingness as the supporting ground of existence. I feel held, "meant" and integrated. In the abundance and vastness around me and within me – often almost impossible to separate – the mind expands, becomes more extensive and at the same time more mysterious. And I mean this primarily ontologically and not just psychologically.

Summer begins when the position of the sun, day after day, is already pointing downwards and darkness is drawing closer and closer. Strange, really. The well-known "delay of extremes". But it does not explain the phenomenon in depth. The density and beauty of manifested being harbour its transience, the "no more", which then becomes "not yet" in stages. The passing of summer and in summer is perceived particularly painfully.

Summer is characterised by a quality of relaxation, calmness, embeddedness, wihout the pushing urgency of spring-time.

Spring seeks form, pushes for form, longs for form, while summer unfolds and exudes it with aplomb. And thus flaunts and glows, even when the magic of the flowers gradually fades.

And shape: What is it? How is it created? From what depths does it emerge? Natural science knows nothing about it. It capitulates to life as such – although the opposite is often claimed – just as it does to consciousness.

Or is the question already nonsensical? There are songs that sing about summer, whereby one starts with the lyrics. But that's not what's meant in the first place. It's about the music itself and its linguistically unfathomable quality. It's about music that breathes big and captures the light and expanse as well as the dark depth and sadness that is woven into almost everything as a shadow that even the summer glow cannot make disappear.

Schubert's great C major symphony is perhaps one of them, in which the landscape around Vienna also resonates and resounds. Grinzing, the Kahlenberg and all that. Summer heat in the alleyways of Vienna. And on the Kahlenberg, I once suddenly and surprisingly entered a different state of consciousness. Everything glowed and appeared to be itself – without being induced by drugs. That was in 1972 and lasted only minutes. A whiff, as it were. But the glow that emerged remained with me forever. It was also sound.

In the mountains. The starry sky that I look at and that looks at me. Summer 1964. The beauty of the stars that hides and reveals their mystery. That opens up horizons. I would have and have a lot to say. Sober and drunk at the same time. Several times there was an incredibly large and radiant Venus in the evening sky, the likes of which I have never seen again since the summer of 1964. The great philosopher of the infinite Giordano Bruno was very close to me. I had only just started reading his writings.

I once saw the stars without seeing them directly. I was staying on a farm in the Dolomites for weeks. Suddenly, in the early hours of the morning, the ceiling of the room in which I was sleeping seemed to open up and a dazzling and stunning starry sky appeared, or rather: suddenly burst in, like a powerful cosmic vision. It was a kind of vision. Then, during the day, I felt immeasurably expanded, vast in an expanse that could not be measured. Later, in the summer of 1986, I also experienced this in the Trans-Himalayas (Nepal, Tibet). But the basic tone was different. Back in Berlin, this had a long-lasting effect. It changed me.

We are also space beings. "Space is the soul of the world," says the great natural philosopher and cosmologist Helmut Krause. A marvellous word, barely fathomable. A mantram perhaps. Once the door to the world soul space has opened, even just a crack, it cannot be closed again. Somehow this also has to do with the summer of the soul. "Summer of the Soul"? Is that more than just a flowery metaphor? I think so. It touches on the problem of language. How far does it reach, what is it capable of or not? It's impossible to think that through to the end.

The quiet waiting, the agreement: It can unfold more easily in summer. Agreeing with what? With yourself first. That is probably the beginning, from which everything else follows. The world around us unfolds from the depths of selfhood.

The deeper we understand and grasp ourselves, the more worldly we become. This transcends and at the same time preserves the I, which is so familiar and yet so abysmal.

By allowing my I to flow into the world, I enhance it and at the same time open it up to the higher, even cosmic We, without it collapsing in and of itself. The I without a higher We and You is pathological and becomes a heavy burden, crushing and ruining the individual.

"In your breast are the stars of your destiny", says Schiller somewhat pathetically, pointing out a truth. We are here and outside at the same time, encapsulated within ourselves, so to speak, and at the same time flowingly connected to the world in an incessant, lively interplay. In that summer of 1964, I experienced this for the first time and then also realised what it means to be cosmically and spiritually connected, not separated, not a being-blind self, which is always bleak and futile.

As someone born in the middle of summer, summer – and especially its height and centre – was and is always a challenge for me, because my birth and the span since then come into play. This has to do with reflecting on what is intrinsic to me, which is undeniably present in the soul space on the day of birth. The old questions are then always looking for new answers. This is also often the case elsewhere, but the days around my birthday, which I often spend travelling, are particularly charged, which can sometimes be difficult, as you will understand. I then ponder more than is good for me.

Summer expands the soul – if there is no extreme weather that endangers the body – but it also draws attention to the small and close, which is more recognisable than usual in the abundance of sunshine. The formal language of natural things cannot be exhausted. The near and small correspond with the distant and large. One determines the other, is reflected in the other, indeed is the other.
The vastness becomes closeness, and the closeness becomes

vast, immeasurable, mysterious. Everything moves, as it were, into its own being, from which it then radiates out into the open expanse that surrounds us and also carries us.

Once again: man is also a faraway being, but the closeness makes the distance bearable. He needs both.

There are summer hours that stretch endlessly, as everyone knows. Sometimes the body can seem to dissolve, almost disappearing in the shimmering light and air. I once lost myself, so to speak, during a Zen meditation outdoors in the summer. I had the feeling that the gentle wind was blowing through me, that I was offering it no resistance, that I – as a contoured self – was disappearing, simply disappearing, quite unspectacularly, as if it could not be otherwise. And yet it was incomprehensible, a mystery for which I had no explanation. Disappearing without disappearing, being there and at the same time "just being gone" for the physical self-perception ... I have always avoided seeking an explanation here or exaggerating the whole thing mystically and speculatively. Why should I?

Summer has countless faces and facets. And yet there is something pervasive, elemental, something that grips the individual in its entirety, which people "normally" cannot and do not want to escape. But it is precisely this normality that is at stake if you allow and can allow what happens inside and outside, if you tune into the great breath that determines summer. This presupposes that there are no inhibiting factors determining the field, as is usually the case, so that certain basic perceptions cannot come into their own. What I write here can then easily be perceived as beautiful and somehow non-committal or quasi-poetic talk that believes itself to be exempt from the hardship and confusion of everyday life. Nevertheless, I would like to take the liberty of presenting a few philosophical and meditative reflections here, beyond the monstrously celebrated madness that reigns everywhere and, as we know, has this earth in its grip almost entirely.

"The worst thing: / Not to die in summer, / when everything is bright / and the earth is easy for spades," says a poem by Gottfried Benn. Why actually? Because the light conceals death, which bursts out everywhere, relentlessly, strictly, following Ananke (ancient Greek, English, inevitability). Isn't there also an abundance of light that contains death, even invites it?

It's not just spring that's a challenge, as I've written before, summer is too, just in a different way.

Spring's plant growth and weaving in its urgent, expectant tension has now, as it were, temporarily become a state of being. The diversity of forms is more or less at rest, remaining in abundance, as if there had never been anything else.

The things of nature have arrived at themselves, and as such they work and radiate. Soon, very soon, they are covered in the first signs of decay, which then become ever stronger.

But this radiance and activity has its own power of being, which many also sense, to varying degrees, and which is associated with meaning and a higher order. To completely abandon meaning and higher order in natural existence, in the transhumanist utopia of a technically interconnected human being in the service of the Megatechnical Pharaoh, is a powerful ideology today that bears fundamentalist traits. Referring back to the natural world seems downright suspicious and is labelled with negative terms. This comes to light openly and often harshly and is one of the battlegrounds in which we are all embroiled today. Whether we like it or not, we become combatants here. Natural being, enhanced to spiritual-cosmic being, versus technical being as the abolition and dissolution of the actual human being as a creative self-being. These are the front lines.

This little summer meditation is also a kind of confession, a confession of the living and its spiritual and cosmic anchoring. And I feel called to tirelessly recite this "confession", even if I sometimes have the feeling of being the famous "preacher in the desert".

* * *

The Melancholy of Nearness to Death

I once described autumn as the "eschatological season" in a previously unpublished text. What does that mean? Eschatology is the doctrine of the so-called last things and of the end times, the final upheaval of human history, usually understood as a promise, as the overcoming of everything that often makes life a torment for us, takes away our creative breath and humiliates and malignantly oppresses us.

When someone like me (born in 1944) conjures up autumn, it makes sense to talk about the famous "Autumn of Life" – which I have perhaps already left behind me. The "many autumns" in the line of poetry by Gottfried Benn, whom I greatly admired at the age of 18/19 – and still appreciate today – are meant differently than I want to imply in the title. Benn is talking about the autumns that "judge summer's happiness", as it literally says, and sweep away everything that moves and fulfils people in terms of genuine happiness and joy, but also in terms of vain arrogance and self-conceit. And this in the knowledge that all this cannot, indeed must not, remain!

Some autumns of my life rise up before me as if blown up from the "well of the past", according to Thomas Mann. They are images of the past that abruptly shine through the brightness of the present, challenging it, so to speak. The old – which is and can never really be past anyway – outshines or drowns out the present, which presents itself so full and dense as if all of yesterday simply did not exist, which, as everyone knows, is a delusion.

Perhaps the saddest autumn song I know is Gustav Mahler's "Lied von der Erde (Song of the Earth)" with lyrics by Hans Bethge. It is entitled "Der Einsame im Herbst (The Lonely One in Autumn)" and begins with the beautiful line "Autumn mists billow bluish over the lake." And towards the end it says: "The autumn in my heart lasts too long ..." You have to listen to the music. I will spare myself the trouble of describing it; that would not do it justice.

There have been great moments of grief in my life that, as in the song, seemed "too long". Far too long. But they were always a challenge that I demanded of myself to overcome, even if I didn't always succeed. But the effort alone had a soothing and clarifying effect.

The month of November "has it all" if you really open yourself up to it, if you understand its song, the song of transience and the proximity of death. As a real, melodically resounding song, it simultaneously conceals and reveals the "sound of the world", the sound of eternity as it were – and not just "as it were" – and of the spiritual-cosmic "being bearing meaning " as the antithesis to the "you-are-devoid-of-meaning-universe" celebrated day after day in the prevailing intellectual culture. Enduring this madness is more difficult in November than in the sunshine of summer. In November, it seems, space, imagined as bleak and empty, breathes particularly coldly on us, even if it is actually an almost pathological fiction that is believed worldwide. Actually puzzling. And then again not ...

October is often still "Indian summer", so to speak, if the cold paw of the previous winter does not show itself too early. In the current situation, this cold paw can have devastating effects, as is easy to foresee. There are clearly identifiable culprits. The old and established term "Indian Summer" will probably have long since been banned by the ideologically motivated language correctors or will soon be. This is only mentioned in passing. In any case, the autumn of October displays a wealth of colour and design of unique splendour. A feast, so to speak, for photographers, painters, writers and others, if they are still open to such phenomena of nature and their sublime beauty, even majesty, which has something awe-inspiring about it.

It is similar here to spring: the colour-saturated autumn overwhelms many people, makes them embarrassed and helpless, because something deeper than the purely visual resonates here. The natural light takes on a very special constellation and intensity, precisely because the days are getting shorter and, as autumn progresses, they seem to dive into the already omnipresent darkness of the universe, in which a different and higher light, an inner light, may be revealed. The question arises as to how the so-called outer light relates to the inner light, if such categories apply to light at all.

Light in general is an abysmal mystery, which even physicists have to admit, although they often give the impression in their public appearances that they are on first-name terms with the spirit of the world and are almost patting it on the back.

The autumnal October light seems to be captured, or rather artfully inserted into the colourfulness of the shortening days, before November increasingly takes over and makes the colours disappear. The great defoliation sets in and advances mercilessly and unstoppably. I'm talking about "our latitudes" here, of course. You have to face up to it. It changes the state of the soul in many ways. And that can certainly take on sinister and frightening traits. Somehow we are robbed; we lose something. The increasing withdrawal of the fullness of light can seem like a threat:

The great darkness could swallow us all up like one of those ominous and, in my opinion, purely fictitious black holes. The famous photo of a black hole, which caused a furore at the time and was probably thought by most people to be real, is more or less a Photoshop-like construction. What is really seen cannot be reliably determined.

The visible loses its power. Can the invisible, which works and weaves behind and within everything, now prevail? It could do so, but it usually doesn't because modern/post-modern man has difficulty withstanding this tension in his soul and tends to flee from it or drown it out or cover it up with technology and media.

The seasons in general have a powerful impact on our lives; they are cosmic rhythms that we cannot avoid, even if we resist them. It's like death. In general, the seasons of the year also reflect the human lot, the inescapability of natural cosmic processes that take hold of us and reorganise us, challenging us comprehensively. Until physical death. And probably even beyond. At least there are indications of this that cannot be entirely dismissed.

What does autumn do to us? Does it graciously carry us on in the breath of the great cycle or does it challenge us sharply, not letting us go, almost forcing us to transform ourselves? Both is probably the case.

Is autumn an eschatological season? I already mentioned this in the introduction. I want to come back to that. It seems that we are living in an eschatological time in which – perhaps, perhaps – that great turning point is on the horizon that we both long for and fear at the same time because it will demand a lot from us. An epochal upheaval is clearly imminent. Or is this a phantasmagoria? A pipe dream of many people when madness is raging across the board and no glimmer of hope is recognisable within the prevailing co-ordinates?

These themselves must break apart and constellate themselves anew. That's easy to say, but what does it really and actually mean if we don't just want to cavort in the fantastic and utopian, while the ground that supports us is increasingly breaking away? Who or what holds us up when we are in danger of falling? Not the prevailing major ideologies, which include, or actually primarily include, abstract natural science, which claims sovereignty of interpretation or a monopoly on interpretation, even though it cannot contribute anything to the crucial questions.

At the beginning of October, I was in a wonderful place in Berlin that many people pass by. In any case, you meet comparatively few people there. The four of us climbed a small hill to finally reach a vantage point that allowed us to look out over a swathe, which is also a depression, in the southwest of the hill. What we saw were familiar and at the same time distant and graceful landscapes that stretched out in a delicate mist. We felt somehow "somewhere else", in a spiritual and physical space that flows through us and at the same time surrounds us.

The early autumn light of a late afternoon manifested itself powerfully and in dazzling abundance. Delightful and enigmatic. And also unexpected in this form. Uncontainable in our consciousness, something far beyond us, something powerful that calls up deep – actually rather high – soul layers and brings them to our attention. How can we survive in the face of this height?

"What am I against space?" asks Wilhelm Meister in Goethe's famous novel as he looks through a telescope for the first time and is deeply shaken. This question can also arise on an afternoon like this and in a place like this. It is actually always relevant and probably unavoidable.

As humans, we are almost always, even unconsciously, in the sphere of influence of this question. Can we avoid it? Not really. It touches on the spiritual and cosmic existence of human beings, i. e. what we are in depth or, to a lesser extent, what we could or perhaps should be, if something like a "should" is what it is all about .

When "many autumns condense", as Gottfried Benn says, many things can emerge that are initially concealed or kept hidden.

It simply establishes substance, essence, meaning and responsibility for what belongs to the essential nature of man, if my perception is not mistaken. But this should not be a moral postulate. Such postulates usually achieve nothing. It has to come from within, from our own inner process. It's not about ideology, about "opinions" that are up for debate and can be discussed endlessly and drearily.

When I was seventeen, and in November, I read the novel "November" by Gustave Flaubert. It made a deep impression on me, partly because it combined the erotic with the loneliness of the "young man". Probably for the first time in my life, I understood something of the power and magic of autumn. I understood Eros and the beauty of transience in general. The mysterious appearance of that which does not and cannot remain. The loss of love in autumn is cruel, but healing because it goes so deep; it challenges us to the utmost. Autumn, deeply felt, becomes a bardo, an "in-between state", as described in the "Tibetan Book of the Dead", the "Bardo Thödol". And awakens us.

Autumn, as it approaches winter, is a great wake-up call or warning call that also contains the question of the relationship between the inside and the outside, which cannot be fathomed rationally. It remains a mystery. The cold grid view of science in intellectual culture only recognises the outside. The majority of so-called modern or even postmodern contemporaries have fallen onto the concrete ceiling of the pure outside world. They may suspect that this will ruin them in the long term, but the collective pull in this direction seems irreversible.

The imperialism of the largely desexualised outside world is a tremendous power factor; it is part of what I have been calling for decades the "Megatechnical Pharaoh", the great idol of our time, before whom almost everyone lies prostrate, to whom they constantly make offerings and to whom they – mostly voluntarily! – submit to. It's like the ancient Phoenicians, only "fancier" and "smarter" and more suggestive.

But now to the end of this little autumn musing. The autumn that we are now entering is, on the one hand, the old and deeply familiar season, but at the same time it reveals what is already on the horizon in an almost treacherous political, powerful, dogmatic and therefore also threatening way. It touches on the eschatological, to evoke once again that which stands there as a promise, as an opportunity. And a "counter-program". "The crisis as an opportunity": that sounds almost trivial and somehow utilised. But there is something in it that transcends this utilisation. And many people sense that. And that's the point.

Do we still have a chance, or are we doomed? We may be in for a tough ride. But there is no reason to resign. Not to surrender anyway. Every delusion eventually crumbles, and then it becomes clear that this is exactly what we have always known. We remember that. In autumn, we realise once again that everything is also memory, anamnesis as a path to knowledge, as Plato says.

* * *

An Epochal Winter Journey

The winter constellation par excellence is Orion. The only constellation I knew as a child, apart from the Big Dipper. It impressed me. In Bali, in October 1995, I saw it lying on the horizon, which seemed strangely foreign Orion occasionally has a stupefying presence, even dominance.

The prevailing cosmology sees the constellations as random configurations of points of light, which are referred to as stars. A rather weak thesis. What are these stars? What do we see when we look at the night sky? Are we looking into a living sphere, which I assume, or into a monstrous celestial desert, devoid of any meaning, devoid of any connection with the fate of earthly things, which is what the prevailing cosmology claims.

The most famous and probably most demanding song cycle in music history. What is the text about? It tells the story of a young man who is driven aimlessly and desperately out into a snow-covered winter landscape because he has lost the girl he loves or has never really "had" her. He plunges into icy loneliness and ultimately into a kind of madness and suicidal behaviour. Wilhelm Müller wrote the text and Franz Schubert composed the unique music. Without Schubert, this poetry would probably have remained without effect.

Why is this song cycle so popular? Because it expresses an event that has a fundamental or archetypal character that also encompasses the epochal. It sings about our epoch, captures it, gets to the heart of it. "The Epochal Winter" is the title of a book by Swiss psychiatrist Hans-Peter Padrutt, which attempts to interpret our time through Schubert's "Winterreise (Winter Journey)". This was long before corona, but has become increasingly topical since then. The "Winterreise" is not over yet. We don't know when it will be.

Madness and death need not be the last word in the face of the world crisis we are facing. We cannot avoid it. It is omnipresent, pervades us, and much more so than most of us are willing or able to admit.

We have become travellers, set off into an uncertain winter landscape, a world of cold and isolation, of perceived meaninglessness everywhere. Where is the way out? What would we have to do to at least prepare for it?

When I think of the political winter, around 2020/2021, dark images come to mind, such as a squad of police officers rushing in to disperse a group of children tobogganing. There was something grotesque and spooky about that. Many thought it was right and "normal". Others – including me – were rather shocked and disgusted at how the state power celebrated itself here, as it often does elsewhere, in a brutal and dull manner.

The famous poem "Vereinsamt (Lonely)" by Nietzsche from 1887 strikes a similar chord to "Winterreise". Only the music is missing. Here it says in stanzas one, three and four of a total of six:

> " The crows cry –
> And fly to the city.
> Soon it will snow –
> Blessed are those who still have a home.
> (...)

The world – a gateway
To a thousand deserts silent and cold!
Who lost that,
what you have lost does not stop anywhere.

Now you stand pale,
Cursed to winter wanderings,
Like smoke,
Always looking for colder skies. "
(...)

This also describes our epochal situation. At least as a possible scenario that is ominously approaching. The winter cold of these times is in all of our limbs. Unless we armour ourselves against it and let the whole thing pass by untouched. This requires a distance that is only available to a few and is not at all desirable.

The "thousand deserts, silent and cold" are probably essentially constructions of a perverted mind that presents itself as having no alternative and wraps itself in the cloak of science. The greatest illusion of the many aberrations of the mind is the "celestial desert", the barren and empty space that turns man into an outcast, a neurotic ghost who calls out into the dead night "up there" but receives no answer. "Is anyone there?" There are more intelligent questions.

The fact that winter, as an earthly season, can also have a threatening effect on life is an elementary experience, which has been captured magnificently in literature in the snow chapter of Thomas Mann's "Zauberberg (Magic Mountain)" novel, to name just one example. Here, the hero or anti-hero Hans Castorp gets lost in a thick snowstorm; he loses all sense of direction. Finally, in extreme exhaustion, strange visions rise up in him in the eerie and at the same time suggestively enticing proximity of death. Eventually, he tires himself out. When it finally clears up and the driving snow ends, he makes his way back to the village.

Winter is the antithesis of summer. Perhaps, if a light-hearted apercu is permitted, there are only these two clearly defined seasons. Spring and autumn are "in-between seasons", indefinite and becoming or passing, in one direction or the other. Summer and winter in our latitudes are giants that stand with their shoulders firmly planted in being, so to speak. In the here and now, difficult to overturn, they hold their ground, despite the floods that jeopardise the solid and ultimately dissolve it completely. Spring cannot be stopped and neither can autumn. It goes on and on, on and on. Or does it?

With philosophically tinted winter memories, we can perhaps approach the very own majesty and mystery of this season, if it can unfold without brutal and hostile interventions within the framework of the dominant mega-technology. The winter constellation Orion has already been mentioned. Somehow, as a child, I saw it as a living magnitude of being, without being able to define and grasp it more precisely.

Today, for a long time now, Orion has been a symbol of cosmic life that I can use as a reference point. With Orion and Sirius, the central star of the Great Dog, in view, I feel enigmatically gazed at from there. Living things meet living things. This has nothing to do with either conventional astrology or so-called modern cosmology and its projections, which are presented and applauded as reality.

I have always loved the beauty of the real and, so to speak, always meant winter, although the inherent danger did not escape me. The two go together. Even small amounts or thin layers of snow have an enchanting effect. Even trivial artefacts suddenly seem to come to life. The entire kitsch industry also makes use of this charm and spoils it in the process. We are living in the era of the great bastardisation anyway. Few things are spared.

One of the most haunting winter experiences of my life was a walk with the philosopher Helmut Friedrich Krause in December 1964. As we approached his home on our return, a heavy snowfall set in, completely covering us within a short time. Our conversation centred on the truly profound question of immortality in a spiritual-cosmic context. The starting point were verses by the ancient Greek poet Pindar, which conjure up something like a mythical immortality. Snowflakes danced around matt shimmering lanterns. Everything seemed muffled. Like a silence that spread out and enveloped us completely. The words spoken took on an aura all of their own.

Two philosophers in it. One was 60 years old, the other 40 years younger, a philosopher in the making, so to speak. I didn't dare to call myself a philosopher until I was 30. Snow magic and immortality. Unforgettable to me. The scene had something literary about it, perhaps even cinematic. A kind of Magic Mountain episode.

A year before this walk – the philosophical and human contact with Helmut Krause only came later – I walked alone for a long time, restless and agitated through snow-covered streets that seemed strange to me. I felt lonely, always searching and as if driven. I read a lot of Nietzsche and

Gottfried Benn, but neither could help me existentially. How could they? This late-night wandering also had something literary about it. It was then reflected in a prose sketch that tried to give form to what I had experienced inwardly, which I only succeeded in doing inadequately. I only got to know Schubert's "Winterreise" later, although I lived through it unconsciously.

Looking ahead to the coming winter of 2022/23, I have rather gloomy thoughts. The prevailing political theatre seems surreal. The leading actors seem somehow grotesque and demonic at the same time. Outrage and a spirit of resistance are stirring in every "human feeling breast" beyond the stultification and stupefaction caused by corona, climate hysteria, war and de facto nihilism.

Anger builds up inside me. Who is ruling over us here? Can we put up with this? Are we powerless? I don't really believe that, I never have. The sharpest weapon at our disposal is, first of all, the mind and its inherent cognitive ability, our own uncompromising thinking, which is also a feeling and perception. The human being has the potential to be a cognisant being. Or is that already too idealistic? That is possible, but what alternative is there? Thinking is a living and creative force if it does not exhaust itself in stupid sophisms or in blind kowtowing to the powerful in science and politics.

Sometimes I think, although it sounds cynical, that many earthlings will fall for almost any madness if it is presented cleverly enough. And often this madness doesn't even have to be skilfully packaged. Even the most undisguised and directly presented insanity is often enough to cloud one's own thinking or to completely disengage it. There is no shortage of current examples of this.

In the legendary winter of 1978/79, which piled up mountains of snow and brought trains to a standstill, I flew from Berlin to Hamburg in response to an invitation.

Let's be honest, it wasn't easy back then, because the runways at the airports and the aeroplanes themselves were covered in deep snow. I remember that it took a long time before we were finally able to take off, freed from the snow. On the flight itself, there was an ambivalent feeling: on the one hand, the fear that the aircraft we had entrusted ourselves to could be damaged by the extreme weather conditions and endanger us. On the other hand, there was a kind of blind faith in the famous power of technology. I talked to my neighbour on the plane about this almost unresolvable dilemma. He essentially agreed with me. I arrived safely in Hamburg and was relieved, but also apprehensive.

Incidentally, meteorologists were talking about a second ice age at the time. The media greedily seized on the topic. Who's surprised? Greed today is focussed on other things.

And as for the freezing that is now so much talked about, I remember a period in the cold and snowy winter of 1987/88 when the heating in my flat broke down. I got through those days with all kinds of tricks, which I don't want to update here for obvious reasons. That was still ideology-free back then. Today, any rubbish can become an ideology.

The largely snowless, cold and wet winters are becoming more frequent. The enchantment then also stays away. Everything remains as dull as many people feel when they are thrown back on themselves and don't want to be anaesthetised by any events or delusions.

In Berlin back then, "in those days" – until when, actually? winter was usually snowy from mid-January to mid-March, rarely as early as December. You could rely on that. I often froze, both as a child after the war and as a student in an attic room that was scorching hot in summer and menacingly cold in winter. I was always busy. That heated me up, so to speak, and helped me. Philosophy worthy of the name – and many "philosophers" fall through the cracks – carried me through everything, fulfilling and fascinating me, just like great music. "Without music, life is a mistake," says Nietzsche. And without real philosophy, too. And without love too, I add here as if in passing ...

I read Schopenhauer for the first time in the winter of 1967/68. It was probably a normal winter at the time. Philosophy and music were what filled me. I added Schopenhauer to the list of thinkers who moved and influenced me: Heraclitus, Giordano Bruno, Schelling, Goethe, Nietzsche, Helmut Krause ...

What follows the "Winterreise", also understood as an epochal phase? The text speaks of madness and death. The music has left both behind. Schubert's music at that time did not culminate in a song or a symphony, but in a string quintet, which many of his admirers consider to be the greatest chamber music work of all. So will the "Winterreise" be followed by the sound magic of the string quintet? What would that be in epochal terms? That would be the great turning point, the great fulfilment, the overwhelming yes of spiritual-cosmic fulfilment, of which it is actually impossible to speak in advance. And that is why it should not happen here.

How does the string quintet relate to Orion, to cosmic life in general? The epochal winter will not be the last word in

the history of these earthlings. But the future cannot be
tapped; it remains in the twilight of a still unfulfilled promise …

* * *

Realisation
and
Science

"A world without life and consciousness
is a delusion."

Jochen Kirchhoff

The Newfound Splendour of Things

It was not only during the corona-virus crisis that it became apparent that science was becoming increasingly religious and at the same time dogmatically entrenched. An occasionally grotesque cult of science was practised, which was displayed like a monstrance.

This had already existed to some extent earlier, actually since the establishment of abstract natural science in the 17th century. But the corona-virus pandemic topped this and exposed it at the same time. It was increasingly less about science in the classical sense and more about kowtowing to the state, i. e. ideology and dogma.

Even clever critics of the corona measures found it recognisably difficult to see through the fetish nature of science – usually understood as natural science. Science itself remained the glittering idol that almost everyone served and admired. Raising serious doubts here was hardly possible or was considered more or less absurd. Anyone who seriously touched on the ideological core substance of science or questioned it quickly found himself confronted with murky suspicions. An icy wind blew against those who tried to dismantle the idol.

These are all familiar things; it is nevertheless useful to emphasise them once again. The reason for this is that contemporaries in the prevailing intellectual culture believe they are on safe ground here, which they cannot and will not leave. When it comes to real knowledge of the world, it is believed that only science in its mathematical-abstract power is capable of making solid and verifiable statements.

Everything else is regarded as dubious and speculative and quickly falls into the category of crankery and sectarianism.

What is science worthy of the name? Can it be conceptualised and defined with any clarity? And: What prerequisites and premises are required for a research endeavour to be considered scientific? First of all, it is important that such premises exist at all, that science is not without presuppositions. These premises define certain guiding principles, which then also influence the results achieved in each case. Anyone who does not accept these premises or sets different ones will arrive at different results.

Science is a method of gaining reliable knowledge of nature using a primarily rational and reproducible approach which is guided by mathematics and experiment. The results obtained in this way are regarded as solid and well-founded findings, which are not about something like ultimate truth in the metaphysical sense, but about mostly abstractly formulated assumptions about the reductionistically trimmed outer world without an inner world. The scientific approach is subject-blind. It has nothing to do with life.

Ultimately, it is about the abysmal question: What is reality? Because this must always be assumed. It is not possible without this large framework of reality. What is assigned to this collective term and – importantly – what is not? This means that not every phenomenon is considered worthy of science, so to speak. Why is that? Because it is assumed from the outset that certain phenomena are not considered real, even if many people judge them to be so based on their experiences.

In 1997, I gave a lecture at the Urania in Berlin entitled "Rebirth as a scientific hypothesis?" This lecture was well attended and moved many people. As I was already established as a "serious lecturer" at the Urania, I could afford to address this sensitive topic directly. (The lecture is available as an audio recording and can be accessed on my Youtube-channel). In posing the question, I – implicitly – assumed that something like reincarnation could actually exist. This premise was accepted by the Urania management, i. e. deemed worthy of scientific consideration. In other words, it was not dismissed as esoteric nonsense in advance, which could have been done. But it didn't happen. Which is not to say that reincarnation has now been elevated to a topic worthy of scientific study. My example was more of an exception. It is clear that I was not in a position, nor did anyone expect me to be, to definitively prove reincarnation as real or as a windy hypothesis. It remained in limbo. That was the best I could do.

The situation was quite different in spring 2000, when physicists had proclaimed the "Year of Physics" and wanted to celebrate it in style. The Urania was the perfect venue. The famous Big Bang was then cheerfully celebrated as a kind of happening with top-class speakers on the podium. Ranga Yogeshwar acted as moderator. The organisers assumed from the outset that something like the Big Bang had actually happened. Not a critical or somehow sceptical word was heard in the run-up to the event.

I had not been invited to the podium as a Big Bang sceptic; the organisers knew nothing about that, but as a philosopher who also deals with physical topics and had become known through a few articles in magazines. When I was invited to speak, I labelled myself, half ironically, as an agent provocateur. The panellists seemed a little irritated, as did the moderator, although he got back on track relatively quickly. But the point of the whole event, i. e. the self-confident celebration of the Big Bang for the "Year of Physics", was now gone.

The event as a whole had been recorded. When I wanted to post the recording on my channel years later, I was forbidden to do so. No reason was given for this. You can guess why this happened ...

The Big Bang was and is officially regarded as a subject worthy of science, which I have never accepted. I am of a completely different opinion. For me, this popular idea was and is a quasi-religious idea, based on a fiction that cannot be proven per se because the conditions for it are not given.

This leads to an important distinction that usually goes unnoticed because most astrophysicists and astronomers are not concerned with epistemological factors that require sophisticated thinking that transcends mathematics.

You could perhaps put it like this: he who thinks does not calculate, and he who calculates does not think.

You can doubt this, but it does not solve the problem at hand, nor does it even adequately describe it.

Ideally speaking, there are three types of natural science: science that is entirely or predominantly empirical, i. e. based on experience. And then there is science based on hypotheses, i. e. science that cannot do without principles guiding knowledge beyond pure empiricism, which are regarded as working hypotheses, i. e. as assumptions that precede all research and searching and lead to more or less good approximations.

Finally, as a third category, there is a purely fictitious natural science, which fills the dark spots of its own view of the world with fictitious quantities that are unprovable. Contrary to what is commonly claimed, these contain the largest part of scientific research. Of course, there are also mixed forms. But the main emphasis is usually clearly recognisable.

In all of this, the basic question must always be considered, which is aimed at the possibilities of knowledge in general and which can be conceptualised as follows: Is the world as a whole rationally recognisable or even reliably describable?

The question can be answered in the negative without great ingenuity. Both space and time, as well as consciousness, the root cause of matter, gravity or cosmic motion and much more are intellectual abysses and sphinxes that hopelessly overtax the human mind.

Thus we live in an incomprehensible system of mysteries and riddles that drags the boldly advancing intellect into the abyss of ignorance.

We live in mysteries, we are a mystery ourselves. Scientifically there is nothing to be gained that is really substantial. This would only be possible from a different depth that merges and intertwines our own consciousness with the cosmic consciousness.

I would like to come back to the premises. Without these premises, higher thinking and research is impossible. Premises also have a value-setting character. I can set the premise that we live in an all-round living conscious and infinite universe, filled with countless inhabited celestial bodies. From this premise, the perception of the world shines and sparkles, as it were. Everything then radiates vibrant liveliness.

We are alive as integral parts and "co-actors" of the living cosmos, which never releases us, but always surrounds us, holds us, flows through us, breathes through us and resounds through us. In the ultimate depth, we are cosmic (spiritual-cosmic) beings who can only gain their human dignity from this. The stunted form of the human being that is usually served to us, moreover in the frame of reference of a thoroughly nihilistic spirituality, is absurd and disastrous.

If man exhausted himself in this, we would be eternally imprisoned in an inescapable farce or burlesque. In the madhouse of a senseless, joyless and essentially demonic world. This world does not exist, has never existed and never will.

It is a phantasmagoria of a thoroughly perverted and sick mind that threatens us and almost drives us mad. This is not how the world looks. Not like this, dear readers. And you know that in the depths of your living being, whatever "science" says about it.

Abstract natural science still is the fundamental and leading science of our intellectual culture, without which nothing works and which permeates everything. As it is quite successful, especially in technical terms, countless people lie on their stomachs and worship it.

They have no idea that they worship, even idolise, their own projections. And they have no idea, that these projections are ruinous, that they lead to a dead end, that they are simply murderous in the long term. They kill us. Everything that is creatively alive evaporates when it is hit by the poisonous breath of these delusional ideas.

Many contemporaries consider themselves enlightened and critical. They present themselves as self-confident and believe they know what this world is all about. In largely naïve realism – "What I see is true" – they have constructed and technically perfected an artificial world that lacks any magic, that is barren and empty, bleak and deceptive. Surrounded by death, which lurks everywhere. The corona years have taken the fear of death to the extreme. The corona regimes have been tireless in feeding this fear and abusing it politically.

Transhumanism also feeds on this fear. And this is also the fear of one's own (delusional) projections, which one cannot escape, which one is at the mercy of in the all around crushing force at the bottom of the soul, which causes fear and horror.

Of course, you could say that if we leave the supposedly safe ground of Western rationality, which is the defining feature of our intellectual culture, where do we end up? Where does it take us then? Aren't we then drifting in a directionless and uncertain world?

That's why science is so important. We believe we are on safe ground here, to say it again. That of knowledge. What people believe and think recedes into the background, indeed becomes irrelevant to begin with. For the most part, this knowledge is not existential or rooted in human experience, but in the cold realm of mathematics and abstraction.

Galileo Galilei was the first scientist to completely ignore living reality in all its complexity and instead establish a realm of spirits that enables power-based access to the world and can do without life. Reality is described merely mathematically. It is never explained and derived from a causal vitality.

What counts and works is the lifeless object, the extended thing that knows no inside, i. e. is simply dead and is viewed as such. Anyone who sees the world in this way will sooner or later end up in nihilism and be crushed by his or her own projections, which form an iron ring around us that we constantly feed with our living energies. If we were to withdraw these energies from it, the whole monstrous building would collapse like a house of cards.

Only spiritually and in the deepest sense of the word physically this world is to be accessed. Then we would realise that we, as living beings, have emerged from an all-round living world and are dependent on it every second. A world without life and consciousness is a delusion. And the prevailing natural science serves this delusion.

For decades, I have been trying to prove to the public that we can look at the phenomena around us – and ourselves – in a completely different way. And I can certainly claim a certain degree of success. Hardly more than the famous drop in the ocean, however. But the first steps have been taken ... If you approach the subject, you don't have to start from scratch.

A major shortcoming of the prevailing view of the universe is that the matadors of astrophysics and astronomy more or less consider themselves to be the pinnacle of earthly intelligence, while at the same time clinging to unintelligent premises that have long since turned out to be fictions.

Foremost, there is a methodological atheism, which assumes that in some sense divine factors do not exist or cannot play a role, for example as principles of explanation. Then there is methodological nihilism, i. e. the fundamental denial of the deeper meaning of the cosmos. According to the motto: This meaning does not exist and therefore should not exist. Furthermore, we have to do with methodological geocentrism, which simply states that everything "there", in the vastness of space, must be or look exactly the same as here on the surface of the earth, minus the life that exists here (strange inconsistency).

This implies an ultimately mysterious wasteland that reduces everything to the dead. We are always the ones looking into space: It is rigorously denied that we, for our part, are or can also be the ones gazed at. This comes from methodical monotony and lack of ideas.

It means that everything becomes somehow banal or trivial. Light is emitted from glowing spheres of gas. This eliminates more subtle approaches to the explanation and derivation of cosmic light, such as that of interlocking spatial energy fields, which only produce cosmic light when they interact with each other. Finally there is the narrowing down of consciousness instead of understanding it as the universal factor and effect of a world soul, as Giordano Bruno, Friedrich W. J. Schelling, Helmut Krause and Jochen Kirchhoff saw or see it. And many others.

Even if these factors, which could be expanded, are no longer understood as premises, but as the exact opposite of them, the view becomes more vivid.

It becomes bright and really interesting with things showing themselves in new splendour. Suddenly we might realise that we have always known, that we have always been there and always will be. And: that we were never really separate.

And never will be. That the you-are-not-meant universe does not exist. Just as little as the wild nonsense of a cosmology of the dead and senseless that has tormented and ruined us long enough.

Everything could be completely different from what the prevailing cosmology claims. Everything is completely different, we are different. The sky above and within us is completely different. We are breaking through the delusion that has held us in its grip until now. We push forward into the vastness. We become essential and substantial. And all materialistic cramp falls away from us. At last, at last ... We become essential and open ourselves truly to the universe. ... Who knows where it will take us ...

* * *

Realisation and Delusion.
The Problem of Science
in the World Crisis

We live on the surface of a sphere that is hurtling through the cosmic night at considerable speed. Whatever happens, whatever we do and fail to do, experience and suffer, build and destroy, etc., takes place on this hurtling sphere, on the "spaceship" Earth. It seems that the majority of Earth's inhabitants have somehow removed their immediate or wider cosmic surroundings from their consciousness. There are day and night stars, other celestial bodies orbiting, there is cosmic light and darkness, the radiant majesty of the day and the occasionally unsettling majesty of the night. However, neither is regarded as an ontological dimension of being with its own dignity and depth, but rather as an ultimately anonymous, blindly occurring event that does not require any deeper thought and therefore has nothing to do with anything metaphysical. Or could have.

Although we are inextricably linked to cosmic fields of experience, for most people in the prevailing intellectual culture this plays a negligible role compared to what they consider to be the only important and essential thing, namely their immediate living environment on the surface of the celestial body, their horizon of experience, their desires and will, their suffering and much more. What comes into consciousness as cosmic is at best so-called astrology or the cosmological narrative that the prevailing abstract natural science has transplanted into people's minds and which is now firmly anchored there. This largely dead image of the cosmic environment is like a ghostly foil behind everything that goes on here. Sometimes, and for some, the suspicion arises that something is strange here and has perhaps been interpreted incorrectly or in an abbreviated or one-sided way. But this suspicion is quickly quelled. After all, "science" has explained to us, without any alternative, how we should see the cosmos and how it surrounds us as verifiably real. "Verifiably real"? Is that really true? Isn't it possible to see things in a completely different way? This question is seldom asked, but sooner or later it should come to the mind of every serious thinker.

In what I write here and in what follows, a sense of this completely different ground of departure pulsates. And the problem of science and this world crisis are not only considered immanently or in isolation, but spiritually and cosmically, without me feeling called upon to broadly present the "other view" in my perception and thinking here. Only a gentle background noise, a kind of cosmic murmur without language, underlies this essay and cannot be detached from it. This may irritate some people, but it would be dishonest if I were to conceal this "other view", which could also pass as a kind of working hypothesis ... Yes, it is a working hypothesis, not a phantasm.

Perhaps also a metaphysical premise, epistemologically speaking, a kind of metaphysical positing for which there is nevertheless empirical evidence.

From the very beginning, I also saw the corona-virus crisis as a spiritual challenge. I wanted to understand, also from a philosophical point of view, what it was actually about, "what was being played here". I realised early on that the official narrative couldn't be right. It was comparatively easy to recognise this. There were so many contradictions, inconsistencies, unsupported assertions, nonsensical measures that were declared to be sensible, even necessary, an authoritarian gesture of downright astonishing simplicity and chutzpah under the guise of science and the so-called lack of alternatives, and much more. This was and is confusing at first. How was and is such a thing possible, and on a global scale? How could it come to this?

Much has been written about this. There are enlightening and intelligent observations from which I have learnt a lot. The front of the "corona sceptics" or "critics of the measures" has brought substantial details to light. However, I always had the impression that essential things were not recognised and understood. I am not making this observation lightly or in a know-it-all manner, but based on decades of experience in the field of so-called scientific criticism, which I have presented to the public in books, essays and video contributions. My criticism of the prevailing natural sciences (and this was my primary concern) was and is essentially fundamental criticism. Decades ago, I had already gained the impression that this was lacking across the board, that hardly anyone was tackling this "hot potato". Why? Because if you consistently touch the (ultimately metaphysical) foundations, the mostly unquestioned premises and axioms on which the whole imposing edifice of abstract natural science rests, an icy wind blows against you. The conclusion suggests itself that there is a kind of taboo here. To a certain extent, there is also the understandable fear of making a fool of oneself and being ostracised in connection with this, of losing one's reputation (if one has one) and virtually falling down. I don't need to go into any more detail here.

First of all, I would like to say that I, like many others, see the corona crisis as part of an unprecedented world crisis, which can be understood as a fundamental crisis of our entire being-in-the-world, as a crisis of consciousness, or, as I sometimes say, as a psycho-cosmological crisis, which is causing us all a lot of trouble and, to varying degrees, is also neurotizing us, if we are honest. No one gets through this unscathed.

"Recognise the situation" is the title of an essay by Gottfried Benn from 1944, which I will try to do here in relation to the world crisis "since Corona". Recognising the global situation, even in the complex variety of interlocking factors that are often difficult to understand, seems indispensable to me, although there are of course limits, especially as overarching spiritual factors also come into play, which are usually not taken into account at all because they exceed the narrow horizon of the prevailing state of consciousness and are quickly devalued as "esoteric" or "astrological". I have to take this risk, even though I write here exclusively as a philosopher and a thinker who has endeavoured to gain genuine knowledge for decades.

Back in spring 2020, I noticed that many people were carrying what they considered to be science before them like a monstrance or the famous Ark of the Covenant. It has long been obvious that science has become a kind of secular religion with ex cathedra declarations that are in no way inferior to the pronouncements of church dignitaries. The dogmatic gesture, even in, let's be careful, bold or even windy theses, is occasionally breathtaking and astounding. Incidentally, it is primarily about natural science, which, as a primarily abstract natural science, represents the basic and leading science of intellectual culture, in the front of which the "laymen" often stand in awe and amazement. It is at its best when it comes across as mathematical (and therefore initially incomprehensible to most people), or even better as a computer simulation whose premises and axioms are not provided. (Usually the researchers themselves are not aware of them.) The modern/postmodern contemporary is more or less a believer in science. As a rule, however, he presents himself as a sceptic ("you can't tell me anything"), well informed, capable of judgement and alert.

The reality is often very different, also (but not only) because the possibilities of direct and indirect influence by the media are now so differentiated that the individual is initially overwhelmed and also lacks the criteria to adequately judge a situation that is presented to him as a fact. Especially when it comes to things (and this is usually the case) for which they lack a direct background of experience. The spectrum of each individual's direct experience is very narrow; most of it is read up on, uncritically adopted, taken on board according to one's own ideology or rejected as "definitely wrong". The sea of opinions is immeasurably large. A quote from "Faust" may be a good addition here:

"O happy, he who can still hope
  to emerge from this sea of error!
  What one does not know, is that one actually needs,
  and what one knows is not needed."

Added to this is the power of the authority of personalities and institutions that have a reputation and are therefore considered trustworthy. Setting oneself apart from this and critically opposing one's own views requires a commitment that is usually impossible to achieve and therefore rarely happens. This is a problem that is often underestimated, especially when it comes to science and its assumptions and assertions. What's more, only those who suspect that something is not right, that something is "wrong" here, set themselves apart and feel the need to do so. They then dig deeper and look for weak points that they try to invalidate in order to bring down the entire narrative. It is always important to remember that without a viable alternative, all criticism is up in the air. This does not mean that this alternative now covers everything and can explain everything, but this is often expected. A sensitive subject, so to speak.

These are actually well-known facts. However, the corona-virus crisis has shown and continues to show this like a magnifying glass. There are countless so-called studies on most topics. Anyone who is inclined towards a certain view, however it came about, will only trust the validity of the study that confirms it and reject the others or view them with suspicion. There are also epochal errors, so to speak, that transcend the individual. Once these errors have been accepted and disseminated long enough, they have their own inertial force against which little can be done at first. Anyone who doubts them faces the most severe and sometimes existence-destroying hostility. And it doesn't help much at first if it turns out at some point that they were right.

The history of science is always also the history of collective misconceptions, even delusions, which are stubbornly held on to. It is important to note that scientific "opinions" or "dogmas" cannot be detached from the context of a rather diffuse worldview that is always present. This worldview context does not have to be directly conscious; it can be implicit and often is. This can be seen in major scientific controversies, such as the correspondence between Newton's student Samuel Clarke and Leibniz in 1715/16, which centred on space, time, causality and God, the absolute and the relative. Anyone who reads the correspondence in its entirety, which was conducted at a high intellectual level, will come to the conclusion without any great acumen that both combatants (Clarke for his master Newton) did not deviate one millimetre from the conviction they held right at the beginning. Neither can convince the other of their own point of view. So the game ends in a stalemate, if one is inclined to see it that way. Of course, commentators judge the contest according to their own basic assumptions or from what they think they know.

Is space absolute, i. e. always there, even if it contained nothing (Newton), or does it only exist insofar as objects are present in it (Leibniz)? What is the quality of space? How does space relate to God? Both antagonists argue consistently with the omnipresence of God. Does God exist independently of space, i. e. does it have its own, quasi-extra-divine reality, or does it, i. e. space, actually not exist at all (as the idealist thinkers, Kant above all, assumed)? Etc.

Or the controversy between Niels Bohr, representative of the quantum theorists, and Einstein. Both had a fundamentally different understanding of reality. The quantum-theoretical approach, taken to its logical conclusion, completely dissolves the traditional concept of the object; what remains is something diffuse, nebulous, which can only be grasped mathematically and causally. Einstein argued that "God does not play dice"; at this point he was arguing quite realistically and from the point of view of conventional causality ...

To take what I mentioned at the beginning a step further, I myself start from a completely different understanding of reality than that of abstract natural science. I start from the premise of the comprehensive vitality and deeper meaningfulness of the cosmos. Everywhere is Gaia, one could say in a simplified way. The people on this planet and on countless other celestial bodies are integral parts of the world soul and the infinitely eternal universe. We look into the cosmos, but what is rarely considered is that this cosmos looks back, as it were. Every monologue is shattered by this. We are comprehensively gazed at, even if we believe, when we thrust our powerful telescopes into the nocturnal firmament, that we only have a dead world of objects in front of us, which has nothing to do with us in the depths, which is totally indifferent to us and to whom we are completely unheeding as well.

I am convinced that the "you-are-not-meant universe" of the prevailing cosmology is an illusion. I will come back to this aspect. As living beings of consciousness, we are embedded in a comprehensively living and conscious universe. Life and consciousness arise from life and consciousness. It has never been observed that living things arise from dead material ...

Here it is appropriate to say something about the nature and origin of what was and is considered to be science. This requires a brief look at the history of science. Modern natural science as a structurally abstract search for knowledge emerged in the late 16th and early 17th centuries in response to the challenge of Copernicanism. Copernicus saw himself first and foremost as a mathematician. His substitution of the earth and the sun (to put it simply) contained no reference to the physics of the heliocentric approach. The most difficult and most worrying question was this: If the Earth (and this had to be assumed) is moving at breakneck speed, why don't we notice it? Why is earthly perception, including what was and is regarded as physics, so closed off to this "unleashed earth" in its frenzied course around the sun? Incidentally, this question can still puzzle or confuse us today. Has it been answered convincingly? Not at all, as I believe I have comprehensively demonstrated.

Post-Copernican physics, which was initially regarded as the perfection of Newtonian celestial mechanics (not entirely identical with Newton's own physics, as we know), provided a rather abstract answer. It postulated the physical equivalence of the famous rectilinear, uniform motion (a fiction of the purest water) with the state of rest. This was or is the "relativity principle of classical mechanics". This did not really answer the disturbing question of how the movement of the celestial body and the perceived rest of the ground supporting us on the surface of the celestial body could be harmonised. It still has not been answered in the prevailing physics, like so many other questions that are wrongly considered to have been clarified in the general consciousness.

Since the technology works, many people (most of them probably) believe that not only the physics on which it is based has been proven beyond doubt, but also the abstract natural science that goes far beyond it, including physical cosmology and the hypotheses and fictions inherent in it. This is simply a mistake. The largely empirical basis of physical principles on the earth's surface or in the cosmic neighbourhood in no way proves the most daring theories and hypotheses of so-called cosmology. For example, the Big Bang, black holes, the curvature of space and much more.

Physics, as a mathematical natural science, was in its origin and basically still is today never related to the concretely experienced living world of man, but always to a quasi desensualised, skeletally diluted and in this sense more or less dead world. It was not about life, but about the abstract description of things that have no life of their own. This life of its own also includes consciousness, basically everything that characterises living existence, including colour, emotion and the complex diversity of perception, to give just a few examples. That has now virtually disappeared. It slipped into the realm of the "merely subjective". Not a worthy candidate for the supposedly "objective" search for knowledge or, more modestly, "description of the world". This has created a split that basically tears the living human beings apart and/or drives them into a lifelong schizophrenia.

Extremely so today: "Out there" a more or less hostile world of objects in a monstrous, meaningless universe that hardly deserves the old term cosmos. This turnes people into, as Sloterdijk says, "cosmic idiots". Ultimately, it ruins man if he does not succeed in opening up a viable alternative that can only be meaningfully conceived from a living, consciousness-filled universe, as I have long favoured, following and continuing the thinking of the natural philosophers and cosmologists Giordano Bruno (1548 to 1600) and Helmut Friedrich Krause (1904 to 1973), to name just two of my most important sources of inspiration.
The so-called abstract natural science, as a science of the

dead, is still regarded as the supreme discipline and model of science in general. This also includes what Carl Friedrich von Weizsäcker called "methodological atheism", which is another premise that underpins the scientific project. Individuals are allowed to "believe what they want", but as scientists they have to work in a strictly atheistic and materialistic manner, and in a reductionist manner anyway: overarching psychological and spiritual principles of explanation and action that fill the universe (there are many indications of this) are more or less taboo and are not permitted within scientific discourse. This is regarded as a private opinion without scientific relevance, which makes the individual who expresses it in public seem rather suspect. This has damaged our perception across the board. And it will take an act of strength on our part to set a creative counter-accent here in order to arrive at a different, deeper and more comprehensive understanding of science.

Methodological atheism therefore necessarily includes methodological all-round materialism (= everything is ultimately material), which squeezes all scientific approaches to the world into a tight ideological corset and – necessarily – leads to grotesque distortions that have nothing to do with reality. Thus, in this view, there can consistently only be material or energetic ("quasi-material") factors at work. And these are tracked down in the depths of matter, in the smallest details. Eventually the "researcher" is sucked down into these cave passages of matter, which is accompanied by a kind of mineralisation of consciousness that causes everything genuinely human to fade away. In transhumanism, this becomes brutally clear.

What has been moving into the public spotlight as virology

for the past two years is almost paradigmatic of the dead concept of science that I have outlined. No virology without computer simulation, without mathematical modelling, and this on the basis of abstract premises that turn living people into mere objects for long stretches, into things, into the function of mathematical principles to which they have to submit when the model-like constructions are presented by political powers and the media as the basis for far-reaching interventions in the lives of countless people. Science then often mutates into a fetish, even an idol: the distilled, mostly isolated numbers presented without context take on a ghostly life of their own, which can completely overwhelm "normal people" (if they still exist) and drive them mad.

The dead triumphs; the living gets under the wheels. The technocratic dictatorship hardly allows any room for manoeuvre. At most, graciously tolerated playgrounds are skilfully offered so that the insanity of the whole thing does not appear too obvious.

In the corona crisis, we are experiencing a sometimes heated and ideologically charged discussion about the question: what is real and serious science, and what must be labelled as pseudo-science and therefore rejected? Camps have emerged and fronts have been set up against each other. There are many statements that claim to be based on scientific knowledge and research. The boundaries are often difficult to draw. Study stands against study. You can almost always find a study that confirms your own opinion or at least puts it in the realm of high probability. And the so-called layperson is often confused and frustrated: What is true?

Example: Do viruses even exist? The fact that they have

never been clearly isolated and purified tends to argue against this. But is that a convincing argument? If the famous SARS-CoV-2 virus actually exists, can it be proven beyond doubt that it is causally responsible for the disease known as Covid-19? So are we dealing here with a scientific finding or just a weak, rather tenuous hypothesis, perhaps even a mere fiction? Is the alleged SARS-CoV-2 virus, as some suspect, just a computer simulation? In any case, the colourful depictions of the virus that the "serious media" are constantly and manically spreading and manipulating are pure fantasy products. Nothing like this has ever been seen even approximately with an electron microscope. You end up in a kind of minefield with such questions, especially if their answers are linked to positions of power, reputation or political influence or interpretative sovereignty. Tough battles are fought on all fronts here. The tone is often irritated, emotionally charged, arrogant or defamatory. Everywhere and with astonishing self-confidence, things are presented as facts that can at best be assessed as assumptions or working hypotheses.

Also, more than most contemporaries think, many things are fundamentally beyond scientific grasp. Space as such, to give just one example, is a kind of sphinx in scientific terms, a complete enigma that has plunged every rationalist into the intellectual abyss. The same applies to time, to the ego, to the origin of life, to consciousness ... We are surrounded by riddles and mysteries, compared to which the usual project of science seems both pathetic and megalomaniacal.

It is epistemological naivety of the first order to seriously assume that this world is entirely rationally accessible. Defining the limits of cognitive reason, as Kant attempted to do, is impossible via this cognitive reason itself; to do so, one would need a quasi-divine meta perspective, an absolute cognition, as Nietzsche already argued against Kant. Some further clarification:

There is undeniably such a thing as empirical science, i. e. science based on experience; in addition, there is the incalculably wide field of hypotheses, conjecture, assertions and "mathematised occultism". It is not far from there to the realm of pure fiction. Most people consider the realm of empiricism to be very large, that of hypotheses to be "somewhat smaller", but still sufficiently large, and that of fictions to be rather small. I am convinced that it is the other way round. Little real experience, a lot of hypothesising and conjecture and an incalculably large field of pure speculation and fiction. This is particularly evident in cosmology, whose matadors consider themselves to be the spearheads of terrestrial intelligence. Yet they are not even able to explain how light can move so straight through empty space. Which carrier medium makes this possible? The light ether was conceptually abolished, but what took its place? Nothing, actually. Nothingness, coupled with the word "quantum vacuum", which conveys little substance – a pure fiction. The only way to really get anywhere here is with more subtle concepts of the ether, which, however, transcend conventional science.

I do not presume to always be able to make this differentiation between empirical, hypothetical and fictitious in the final analysis. But there is no denying that this rough tripartite division exists, and it is certainly helpful and a guide to knowledge. Many things I or "one" simply has to accept or more or less believe. Only in relatively few fields can I fall back on my own, truly empirical research. The more abstract, complicated and indirect the respective chain of evidence or reasoning is, the more difficult the whole thing becomes. The basic question "What is scientific evidence?" thus becomes an abyss.

Cosmological questions lack an empirical approach in the true sense of the word; the results are heavily dependent on models and are based on premises that are essentially metaphysical assumptions and whose ultimate justification is impossible. The so-called Big Bang is a striking example of this. It cannot be proven structurally, so to speak, as you can quickly see. If, for example, the so-called red shift, i. e. the shift of the galactic spectral lines towards red, is not interpreted as a Doppler effect (i. e. as a flight of the spiral nebulae, as was said at the time), as Hubble did at the end of the 1920s, but as "light fatigue" or caused by other field effects, then completely different results are obtained.

The fact that I am drawing on cosmological elements here is not only from an epistemological or critical perspective (as important and interesting as this aspect is), but also from the perspective of the human-cosmos question, which is of almost unfathomable anthropological relevance. And this also addresses the image of man. What is the nature of man? This (metaphysical) question is usually dismissed as too speculative. One gets the impression that political, sociological and scientific processes on our home planet can, indeed should, be considered completely independently of overarching cosmic or rather cosmic-spiritual factors, and that they are immanent, so to speak. I think this is a huge mistake.

The prevailing cosmology turns man, the "earthling", into a

quasi-nothing, a being whirled up senselessly out of the night of non-being, with whom there is "nothing about at all" in the deeper sense. And which chases towards its death as a black, crushing wall, before which most people freeze in fear. The anthropological and cosmic nihilism here is palpable. Anything that goes beyond this is regarded in public discourse as mere opinion, as ideology, as "merely subjective" without anchoring in solid, material and rationally determinable factors. This touches on the aforementioned methodological atheism, one could also say methodological nihilism, methodological meaninglessness. For decades, I have also been talking about "subject-blind science", which has not been abolished or overcome by quantum theory, as is often claimed. The abstractionism of the prevailing physics, which is far removed from life, even hostile to life, is virtually crowned in quantum physics. It is strange that many do not realise this. Quantum theory cannot really explain any natural thing, be it an ant, a blade of grass or a human being, insofar as it is nature.

The conflicts of our time cannot be resolved in the context of this methodical nihilism, this pure and bleak immanence without a spiritual-cosmic anchorage. This is all too clear to see. The majority of people on this earth in the prevailing state of consciousness, the intellectual culture, feel like meaningless flotsam in the sea of a dead outer space that breathes on them coldly and mercilessly. The "world soul project" is considered to have failed across the board (Sloterdijk). The "cosmic idiot", which has already been mentioned, is then the only possible and scientifically approved form of human existence. The so-called dignity of man, which is ultimately metaphysically anchored, then falls by the wayside. This can be seen everywhere in its consequences. The majority of so-called modern or postmodern people have fallen onto the concrete ceiling of the material outside world. The pure here and now, the pure, materialistically conceived immanence destroys or shatters in the medium term everything that constitutes the core substance of the human being. Here man must become a neurotic spectre, with a panicky fear of death. That this is the case is obvious enough. The corona-virus regimes play on this nihilistic fear of death with shameless sophistication.

Transhumanists are on the rise because there is no creative and genuinely intellectual counterforce to the all-round sick vision of the human machine. So-called AI (artificial intelligence) is cheered by countless people. Why? Because there is a lack of natural intelligence. Because humans have failed here across the board. I am aware that many people see it very differently.

This brings us back to science and, necessarily, to the image of man. The wrong development here causes the wrong development there. What is the cause, what is the effect? Man has lost himself, you could say. He has delegated his core substance, as it were, to the machine and to the many technical, including digital, idols that he serves. The technosphere has long since become the theosphere and now dominates this maltreated planet across the board. This is not good for any of us even if we think we are benefiting from it while trivialising the idol that is pushing us forward. "You think you are pushing, but you are being pushed", says Faust (Walpurgis Night).

And: the aforementioned "quasi-nothing" human being, how else could it be otherwise, all too often acts as a "quasi-god". "If no god will be on earth, / we ourselves are gods", we are told in "Winterreise" (22nd song). This is obviously the cheerful or even desperate maxim, which is more of a slogan or a battle cry.

In this global crisis that threatens to ruin us all, many are clinging to "science" as if it were the only safe and reliable ground. It is probably necessary to define more precisely what this is actually about. We have already mentioned the original impulse of modern science in astronomy, in the confrontation with the Copernican challenge. To a certain extent, this challenge still exists today. This is because the questions that were raised at that time (contrary to what most people believe) have not really been resolved. The matadors of abstract natural science, of which Galileo was the first, rejected (and still reject, or continue to reject) the question of the essence or inner quality of being of the objects and forces of the world to be researched, in favour of mathematisation and abstract modelling, which does not really explain anything, but gives technically powerful access to the world.

I occasionally speak of the "mathematised occultism" of abstract natural science, to use this term once again. The essence of things remains hidden (= occult) and is of less and less interest, while the functional and formal aspect of the things of nature and the cosmos, which are more or less imagined as dead, almost exclusively dominates the field. Why think more deeply when you can do the maths? Those who can calculate do not think. And those who think do not calculate, at least not with the dead numbers that are taken seriously in science alone. "Numbers kill", says the cultural philosopher Oswald Spengler (who was also a mathematician).

Ideally, the large-scale scientific project is based on the endeavour to gain rational knowledge of the world according to clear and strict principles and criteria, including so-called reproducibility. The basic premise is that rational and empirical knowledge of the world is possible and meaningful to a certain extent. It opens up constantly expanding and deepening perspectives on "the world", in extreme cases on the whole of existing things, the universe (= cosmology). The basis of science should be empirical, i. e. based on objectifiable experience, insofar as this is possible. Much, indeed most of this world eludes direct experience. The indirect dominates the direct. This is rarely reflected upon more deeply, for which there are several reasons. One is rooted in the hubris and megalomania of the scientific mind, whose delusional ideology includes representing the pinnacle of human intellectual greatness, which considers everything and anything to be legitimate before the judgement seat of its own great power, and in any case without alternative. The self-deification of man is openly revealed here. His ignorance is directly proportional to the megalomania he displays.

In the corona crisis, many things have come to light in a woodcut-like manner that have been the case for a long time anyway (I repeat this, like many other things, quite deliberately, for mantric reasons, so to speak), namely the lack of a higher image of man that is adequate to the spiritual complexity and depth of man, and this in close connection with a world view that is in parts downright absurd, a meaningless and dead universe, dominated by so-called laws of nature that are blind to consciousness and function like machines.

We have masked or blocked the comprehensively living and meaningful cosmos with our projections, as it were. This crushes us and also destroys any spiritual-cosmic context of meaning. Without this, however, we are lost. Meaningless flickers of consciousness in the celestial desert, which are blown out after a short lifetime by the storm wind of our own projections, which appear as objective realities.

The materialistic/reductionist view of the world and people is demonstrated in its dullness and hostility to life through corona. All so-called measures, globally, bear this brutal stamp. The epistemological errors and misdirections are palpable. For example, the orientation of "governmental" scientists towards computer models, abstract figures and diagrams with prognostic claims that cannot be connected to the complex living reality of actual people. The justifications offered were and are monocausal and one-dimensional and therefore purely speculative in their basic direction. The disorientated politicians refer to the "expertise" of the relevant scientists, which takes on a quasi-religious status. The famous statement of the church father Tertullian "Credo quia absurdum." (I believe it because it is absurd) has always reminded me of this. But also many other times. Of course, there is also solid and well-founded science, but usually only on a comparatively manageable terrain, where the possibilities of error are also manageable. The situation is completely different when it comes to difficult complexities and causalities that can only be analysed indirectly, if at all. This is where the majority of scientific energy is channelled. At the same time, this opens the door to often wild speculation.

I must add another factor that has not yet been mentioned. We live in a time in which almost everything is somehow morally charged. This is especially true of science, whose ideology actually includes being "beyond good and evil", i. e. beyond moral norms and guidelines. There is little sign of this in the corona-virus crisis. The dispute between scientists is no longer primarily about right and wrong, but about what is ideologically and powerfully supported and desired. The focus is not on the open-ended debate of arguments, but often enough on attitudes, political ideology, the favoured world view and so-called morality. Why actually? Perhaps as a counter-movement against the de facto nihilism of a humanity drifting along in meaninglessness, the majority of whom are driven forward by the glittering metallic idol that I call the Megatechnical Pharaoh, a collective term for the abstract apparatuses of power. The icing on the cake of morality is mendaciously placed on top of the respective madness, and with astounding success. Anyone who believes they are on the right side as a devoted citizen, but also ideologically in other respects, needs the moral posturing to feel good about themselves. "You are jeopardising human lives if you, quite selfishly, don't get vaccinated or walk around here without a mask!" This is a judgement of condemnation that is intended to bring the person addressed in this way to their knees morally, even robbing them of a genuinely human attribute.

How we see the cosmos (world view) has a lot to do with our view of humanity and the way we inhabit the earth and relate to it. Every culture or collective soul formation has its own psycho-cosmology and thus its universally binding internal space that embeds and supports the individual. This binding inner space has been lost in Western intellectual history and cannot be regained, which, if it were possible, would hardly seem desirable. Only within a soulless cyber-space on the backdrop of the cosmic forlornness of the individual an overall unquestioned consensus is still binding ... The connecting element is actually nothingness.

When the starry world is silent, the cosmos comes into view in a monstrously distorted form. The living, interlocking spatial energy fields are no longer allowed to exist in the sea of the world soul, only the black and consciousness-blind outer space remains as a barren endlessness, turning man into a cosmic outcast, trembling in his fear of death and loss of being. Then the mentally "preconceived" desert "out there" is materially reproduced on the surface of the stars. The cosmos has been spiritually destroyed and depopulated and now grins demonically at the earthlings. "The cosmos is like a mirror," is an old Persian saying. "If a donkey looks into it ...", it must also be confronted by a reflection of itself. (I should ask the donkeys, these wonderful animals to forgive me for referring to them in this way). To put it briefly and almost trivially: man sees and evaluates the cosmic and earthly environment according to his own consciousness, collectively and individually.

When the dead cosmology falls, which is unthinkable without a "metaphysical revolution", the megatechnical delusion with all its absurd and anti-life fictions and narratives will also collapse. Then the sky clears, as it were. Man realises that he was never separated, that his exile always has been an illusion. I will allow myself this vision without, as it were, painting it out, at the risk of being categorised as a fantasy author. "I love him who desires the impossible", says Manto in the second part of Faust. But it is important, indeed indispensable, to advance towards a more saving perspective that breaks through the prevailing delusion. How and where can this be found?

Ultimately, all questions of this kind lead to one big question: What kind of world (= universe) do we actually live in? The answer to this question, whether explicit or rather implicit, determines our entire being-in-the-world in all its facets. Are we, the inhabitants of the earth, alone in an absurd universe governed by blind forces and laws, which is indifferent to our weal and woe because we are not even intended, so to speak, but only owe our existence to a somehow crazy twist in the gears of things? Girded by the nothingness from which we come and which will eventually make us disappear again, chasing towards an ultimately senseless death, a cruel prince feared by all, whom we cannot escape and who is always "already there", like the hedgehog and his wife in the famous story of the hare and the hedgehog?

What is behind all this? Isn't the fear of death in its depths a completely different fear, namely the fear of oneself in the extreme confrontation with one's own self, one's own suchness in its spiritual-cosmic anchoring? Who are we ontologically if we are not simply dull schemes or chimeras mocked by chance in every possible way, lurking at every corner (on earth and in space)?

The corona-virus crisis has brought the sense of futility that is rampant everywhere and with it the fear of annihilation through death into collective awareness. What has been repressed on all sides is now coming threateningly close to us. The virus becomes death par excellence. The enemy par excellence. This enemy must be fought with all means at our disposal. And in the merely external world of the materialists, this simply means prolonging life at almost any cost. The human being is reduced to a body only, and this body is mercilessly appropriated, colonised, even patented and pressed into the Great Machine of which it is to become a part. Spirit, soul, creative intelligence, resistant vitality, metaphysical dignity – all of that falls by the wayside and is of little interest. Anyone who thinks more deeply disrupts the machine's process and the transhumanist agenda that is being mercilessly pushed forward.

Science (in the sense of the abstract agenda) is not only becoming a fetish, as already mentioned, but a kind of compulsory event, according to the motto: yet more science; that will help us all. Sooner or later, we will overcome what has plagued humanity so far. Now we are entering the Brave New World, from the smartphone to the smart city, the smart state and, even better, the smart planet. In general, there is constant talk of the planet (of its salvation anyway, which is already being verbally celebrated on T-shirts and backpacks), although, on closer inspection, it counts for next to nothing in its own cosmic dignity. Ultimately, earthlings don't even know which star they actually inhabit.

The smart craze knows no bounds. The chips you get implanted are just the beginning. You yourself become a chip and are then freed from the burden of the flesh.

How do we overcome the materialistic, reductionist and abstract science that is favoured by the majority today? I am primarily referring here to so-called natural science (which only deserves this designation with restrictions), to which all other sciences are ultimately orientated. Criticism of science, as I represent it, is not hostility to science, but a passionate endeavour to gain knowledge of the world, and thus also of a science that focuses on the cosmos and human be-ings in their depth and fullness (and that includes con-sciousness).

The global crisis we are experiencing, which is basically overwhelming us all, cannot be overcome without a radical rethink. That's easy to say, but what does it mean? This re-thinking can probably only take place in a kind of cultural revolution that cannot be planned or produced on the sur-face, but can probably only develop and constellate in the most extreme distress, when the "human project" threatens to fail comprehensively, when "everything is over" or seems to be. Then, in a deeper understanding that includes but transcends the systemic component, a (cosmically induced) "turnaround" can take place that turns many things. And everything is decided by the question of who we are then. This cannot be determined in advance or even demanded. Postulates are useless, as we know. But genuine thinking, in relation to the living reality of the earth and the cosmos, triggers effects. Every living being in its own intensity and fullness of creativity is a counterforce against annihilation, against the nihilistic matrix, which is still triumphant here for the time being and has a firm grip on almost everyone and everything. Resistance to this is necessary, in thought and in action.

Without the spiritual-cosmic perspective, which I have already hinted at without defining it in a more differentiated way, it will not work. Immanently, I believe, we are lost or "screwed". "Only a God can save us", says Martin Heidegger in the famous interview in "Der Spiegel" from 1966. Does that help us? Hardly. Although it addresses something that seems worth considering to me, namely that it is intrinsically not possible, cannot be possible. People on earth, left to their own devices and on their own initiative, will not succeed in breaking through the prevailing delusion. There is at least little to be said in favour of this. The "cosmic factor" must be added, in fact: it must be the initial spark. That would then be the counterpart or equivalent to Heidegger.

Everything is animate, animated and permeated by consciousness. That is my metaphysical premise. Much follows from this. Everything that is animate and animated wants to preserve itself and is willing to defend itself against forces that threaten or even destroy it. We humans, on all inhabited celestial bodies, are players in this drama. Spiritual battles rage around us and within us, if we are allowed to use this terminology. The cosmos is not an idyll in this flat sense, but rather moulded life in the struggle of consciousness.

Everywhere beings struggle for consciousness. Space is not a dead extension of a barren endlessness, but is pulsated by the world soul.. This marvellous word has almost completely disappeared from our vocabulary. The desolation and trivialisation of language corresponds to the mega-technical and abstract formation of consciousness that dominates the globe. How much longer still will this continue?

* * *

The Devil's Labourers

Oppenheimer and the Bomb

With his film "Oppenheimer", Christopher Nolan brought the debate about the atomic bomb back into society. We still don't understand it today. The "Manhattan Project" is the quintessence of modern science.

The atomic bomb is the great angel of death hovering over humanity. It signals and manifests a permanent threat that no one can escape. At the same time, it raises fundamental, even abysmal and agonising questions that very few people even ask themselves. But these are the questions we want to address here.

First of all this: What energy is actually released in the atomic bomb? The whole world thinks it knows. But the matter is more mysterious than many people think. Because what is energy anyway? What is nuclear power? What is nuclear energy? As is well known, physics has never managed to bring about any real clarification here – which incidentally applies to most of its common terms.

"We have done the devil's work," summarised Robert Oppenheimer, the head of the Manhattan Project, looking back on his work. And also: "We have learnt about sin." Insightful sentences that can and should be taken seriously. After all, they refer to one of the greatest crimes against humanity. Has this crime contaminated science in general, and, of course, physics in particular? This was certainly discussed by individuals in 1945 and in the years that followed, but today it plays a rather subordinate role. This should come as no surprise, as the globally dominant mega-technology has already presented itself as having no alternative and has long since put all living things on the defensive.

Transhumanism and the atomic bomb are closely linked, as can be recognised without great ingenuity. They are large-scale projects that are hostile to life, which threaten us and yet are being mercilessly pushed forward.

Natural science since Galileo, it must be remembered, has always been an abstract natural science; it has never been concerned with understanding the living world. Strictly speaking, there has hardly ever been a science of life. Abstract natural science has always been about a quasi de-sensualised, skeletally diluted and, in this sense, dead world. The question of the essence of things was therefore margin-alised. It was considered irrelevant. Why colour, why mean-ing, why beauty, why spiritual-cosmic connectedness? None of that mattered any more. It did not count and was therefore not counted or subjected to the dead number.

What mattered, on the other hand, were things, and therefore objects without an inner side, without qualities, without consciousness. This limitation was the great strength of mathematical physics, which initially became the basic and leading science of modernity. Even quantum the-ory did nothing to change this. Subject-blind science tri-umphed across the board – a science that viewed the world as a mere world of things, as a mere outside. Parallel to this development, the universe increasingly became a hostile desert, accessible and explorable only through the cold and more or less dead grid view. In this context, the technology historian Lewis Mumford once spoke of the "crime of Galileo"; a crime that most people do not see or do not want to see as such. However, as Peter Sloterdijk puts it, man mutated into a "cosmic idiot"... And he has remained in this role to this day.

It is precisely because of this "cosmic idiocy" that abstract natural science was able to reach the heights it has achieved and continues to achieve. And this despite the fact that it ruins us in the medium term. So when the biochemist and science critic Erwin Chargaff, once co-discoverer of DNA, describes the atomic bomb as the "quintessence of natural science", he is making a judgement that can hardly be surpassed in its sharpness. In this judgement, the whole of natural science is heading towards its omega point, and this point is the atomic bomb. It has been said on various occasions that the horror of nuclear devastation signifies the "loss of innocence" of science. But this is a rather naive view. This innocence never existed.

In a long conversation about the foundations of physics that I had with Werner Heisenberg in the summer of 1974, I asked Heisenberg to formulate in just one sentence what he, as a physicist, would describe as his innermost concern. He responded: "I want to understand nature and understand it so precisely that predictions are possible." However, this sentence contains a considerable limitation, a tunnel vision. This is because the fullness of life can never come into focus in this way – nor should it. The universe as a living organism, as the great Renaissance philosopher Giordano Bruno still saw it, thus remains invisible and unrecognisable. And this is still the case today. Even the largest telescopes cannot change this. On the contrary. They only feed the hubris of the researchers involved.

It is therefore only logical that abstract natural science, when given the opportunity, also wanted to open up the micro-world and the radiation phenomena of matter with its analytical tunnel vision. Their aim was always to break open the security lock of nature, i. e. "what holds the world together at its core". It was like a magical pull that drew the researchers into the smallest details of matter and increasingly mineralised their consciousness. The political constellation also did its bit to pave the way for this dark desire.

Thus the atomic bomb is the gruesome changeling of modern abstract physics. Because you can't build a bomb with Newtonian physics. But you can with the means of mega-technology and the abstract tools and mathematical methods that overrun and level everything living. I would like to point out here that the connection between the energy formula popularised by Einstein and the atomic bomb, which has been put forward countless times, was not so direct. Matter was by no means converted into energy "just like that". Ultimately, it remains unknown what really happens during these processes. It is like "mathematised occultism". The substance of the matter largely disappears behind the increasingly comprehensive mathematics practised. Formulas, hypotheses and bold fictions dominated the field. Without maths, nothing worked and still doesn't work. However, this has made the epistemological and philosophical fundamental criticism, which still exists in isolated cases, enormously more difficult.

Yet, what energy really is and how it manifests here (this also applies to matter) remains unknown. A complete transformation of matter into energy has never been observed. And it also does not happen in nuclear fission and chain reactions and their disastrous consequences.

In this context, there is an interesting but little-noticed statement by Werner Heisenberg on the question of the energies released in atomic explosions, which I would like to quote here because it is of central importance: "It has occasionally been claimed that the enormous amounts of energy in atomic explosions arise directly from the transformation of mass into energy and that these huge amounts of energy can only be predicted on the basis of the theory of relativity. This view is based on a misunderstanding. The large amounts of energy ... have been known since the experiments of Becquerel, Curie and Rutherford on radioactive decay. ... The energy that is released in an atomic explosion therefore comes directly from this source and is not produced by the transformation of matter into energy."

The atomic bomb can be understood as the innermost core of natural science and its structurally abstract search for knowledge. In the long term, this approach almost always leads to destruction, even if many people may not want to hear it. Anyone who understands the world primarily as a calculable context of forces will try to destroy it at some point. Only by regaining the living and thus also the living cosmos that supports and surrounds us, do we have any chance of freeing ourselves from this blindness. Perhaps this will require a profound rethink.

At the moment, however, there is nothing to suggest that such a spiritual revolution is possible. The majority of people on this strange celestial body that we inhabit seem to have made themselves at home in a universe that is far removed from life, indeed in parts it seems almost criminal or fascist, in which black holes as star-devourers and similar monsters dominate events. If this is happening above and around us, what can we orientate ourselves by? Cosmology would then actually be chaology, which is also a reflection of our collective state of consciousness. We understand the universe according to our consciousness.

The atomic bomb epitomises people's delusions about the world, which have become firmly anchored in their minds and are regarded as objectifiable science. The mushroom cloud takes on an almost sacred status here. Shiva is destroying the world. And the fear of this is deeply rooted in people's souls. The so-called modern or postmodern human being is a thoroughly divided or schizophrenic being. He inhabits the living world, which still exists in remnants, but at the same time he has almost said goodbye to it. With his consciousness, he has long since submerged into cyberspace or ascended into the orbit, from which the ghosts of his own projections now grin at him. Images from which he cannot escape.

So the devil's work is done. What do we have to oppose it now?

* * *

The Human Being in the Living Cosmos

"The cosmos is like a mirror."

Persian Saying

The World Without Us

It is more or less a foregone conclusion that nature is older than man, after all, it brought man into being and will melt away or shake him off at some point, and its unthinkable flow will continue, on and on, only without man. He will then disappear as if he had never existed.

Many welcome this disappearance of humans, at least in theory or, rather, ideologically. Nature can flourish again when the disruptive human factor that ruins everything is no longer there.

So far, so good. Or not so good. This view implies the meaninglessness of man and that there is nothing more to him. So it would be better if he disappeared without a sound. Nature will thank us for it. What is meant here is, first of all, nature on earth, which floats as an oasis in the sea of space imagined to be dead and hostile to life. Ultimately as empty flotsam with no deeper meaning. Postulating this is considered science, the rest is bad poetry.

If you take the opposite premise, i. e. if you assume that human existence in the universe is meaningful, which in principle should then be the case everywhere, then humans move into a completely different state of being. Life then feels different, vibrates differently, becomes essential, cannot be thought of without cosmic responsibility. The human being becomes an all-round being, indeed, he virtually constitutes the cosmos. The universe is only a real cosmos through and via man, which is comprehensively alive and thus embedded in an infinite and all-living structure of meaning.

But let's first take a few steps back and ask questions that help us to find our location and fill it with life and responsibility. What actually is nature? In ancient Greece, we find a wonderful definition of man within nature. Nature was seen as a complex interplay and juxtaposition of origin (arche), goal (telos), the process of cosmic becoming from the beginning to the end and climax and its inherent meaning. This created a great arc of being in which man was placed and which was rooted in the totality of the thoroughly meaningful cosmos.

For the Romans, there was a shift in meaning within the framework of a natural order of being. The starting point of everything natural was "nasci", i. e. to be born. And this always resonated when talking about "natura". So we still have a living and meaningful concept of nature, which at least contained the last remnants of the ancient Greek cosmos.

The modern movement of thought then established a completely different concept of nature. Nevertheless, the old cosmos was still alive in parts. This was the case in natural philosophy, especially that of the infinity philosopher Giordano Bruno, who conjured up the vitality of the universe like no other.

Western natural science and rational philosophy then postulated "nature" as a mere outside world without an inside, as the stage of our being, which could be measured mathematically and subjected to the cold grid view of the analytical-reductionist mind.

Nature lost its vitality; the technical-imperial spirit triumphed across the board. At some point, everything alive in people's minds evaporated. Nihilism began its triumphant march, which continues to this day.

This shifted the anthropological question, i. e. the question: What is man, in his essence? What is there to suggest that we represent a cosmically intended and meaningful form of being? Many people doubt this anyway, or consider this assumption to be a kind of beautiful spiritual fiction that does not need to be taken seriously.

What we are experiencing on our planet today is a fierce intellectual battle over the image of man that seems to be approaching a final showdown. The faction of "humanity deniers" is strong – I use this term now, semi-ironically, in reference to dogmatic formulas in which the denial of tabooed phenomena comes into play. Powerful battalions have gathered around them, and they will not give in easily.

Their central credo with regard to man can be outlined as follows: There is little to do with man; he cannot be ascribed any kind of metaphysical substance whatsoever. He is a higher animal that inflates megalomaniacally in order to ultimately disappear into a nihilistic nowhere; man is presented as an animated nothingness. Whipped up by delusional ideas and dull egoisms, strapped into the corset of a nihilistic straitjacket that robs him of his higher breath. A necessary counterpart to this straitjacket is the idea of a meaningless, hostile and all-round monstrous universe in which violent phantasms such as the so-called black holes wreak their quasi-fascist havoc. A nightmare ... Strange that there is so little resistance to this, which one would actually expect.

The researchers involved believe themselves to be on a first-name basis with the world spirit and allow themselves to be admired and celebrated accordingly. The transhumanists imagine themselves as the world spirit; they do not serve the world spirit, but are it themselves or rather believe themselves to incarnate it.

The "humanity deniers" ask themselves the anxious question: "Are we alone in the universe?" This question alone has exposed them as "cosmic idiots" – to use a suggestive term from Peter Sloterdijk – because no halfway intelligent person would hold the view that this strange crew on spaceship Earth is racing or floating through space alone and isolated. The anxious questioners fear that they will encounter superior beings who could make them appear ridiculous. Deep down, they know that their intelligence does not reach far, yet they are somehow proud of it. They consider themselves to be the spearhead of earthly intellectual power. Amazing, actually ...

In a way, "humanity deniers" are also cosmos deniers. They deny the metaphysical depth of human beings and of the cosmos itself, which supports and surrounds them. They consider the cosmos to be less intelligent, otherwise they would not favour such absurd world views. Who believes the self-appointed cosmologists? I certainly don't.

The concept of nature can be applied to the universe. Then everything that exists is itself nature. Nature is what man is not if we take him out of the context of nature. This is how it is usually seen.

Is man nature or is he somehow outside of it? How is the whole thing constructed and constellated? If we were only nature, in the sense of the materially tangible world stage, then we would be lost. Then there would be no way out of the celestial desert that is imagined everywhere.

I believe that the human being emerges everywhere in the cosmos under certain conditions, that we are surrounded by an unimaginable fullness of being, which always includes the anthropos, the actual human being. Celestial bodies are the carriers of human life, everywhere and since the abyss of eternity. So humans are eternal beings, anchored in cosmic being, in the infinity of space and time. Eternal, eternal, eternal ... Or, as Goethe says:

"Formation-transformation,
the eternal mind´s eternal recreation."

We grow up on celestial surfaces in order to leave all this behind us at some point, in order to immerse ourselves in the divine primal substance of which we are a part – if this semi-religious formula is permitted here.

Life everywhere, intelligence everywhere, consciousness everywhere, embodied first and karmically formed, having passed through suffering and death. The celestial bodies are carried and permeated by enormous space energy fields, which generate cosmic light by interacting with each other.

We view the universe – how else! – according to the measure of our living consciousness, not according to the measure of technical devices and measuring instruments with which we can never leave the narrow circle of material things and forms. "The cosmos is like a mirror" is an old Persian saying. "A donkey looks into it (...)." I must apologise to the donkeys here for bringing them up like this.

We are not only those who view, nor only those armed with gigantic telescopes, but also those who are viewed, those who are always meant, who (have to) act on an open karmic stage – we cannot hide; what we are is openly revealed.

The majority of earthlings have not managed to penetrate the sensual earthly haze. They were or rather still are unable to grasp the inexhaustible abundance of humanity in the universe. They feel alone and do not realise that they are standing and acting in a glistening light, so to speak, blown about by the storm wind of karma, which can never be escaped. They thrust their telescopes into the black night in the hope of gaining real insights. The projective nature of their research endeavours remains hidden from them.

Man evolves everywhere in the universe out of nature. In a certain sense, he is not a part of nature, but its essence; he incarnates the whole of natural being. And only because this is the case can he evolve towards himself. This leads to questions of cognition of a fundamental nature that cannot be avoided. At the beginning of experiencing the world or being in the world, there is, usually unconsciously, the question of cognition in general. What can be recognised, where do I have secure ground, where am I projecting and so on?

Ultimately, it's about the question of all questions: What kind of world do we actually live in? And: How did we get into it – perhaps we fell into it? Man, says Novalis, is "a source of analogies for the universe". The world thus contains the human being as its integral part, although this being a part in the actual sense does not exist in the depth of existence.

Man represents the whole because he is interwoven into the basic substance of the world and belongs to it. As a cosmic being par excellence, he focuses and bundles the whole and can only therefore recognise this whole in its basic structure. At his core, he only recognises himself because he is the world encompassing being par excellence.

Idealist philosophy, such as that of Schelling, has already differentiated this and presented it in a way that can hardly be refuted: I am the world. I recognise the world because I am it, because I incarnate it and am constituted by it, but at the same time I also constitute it in its entirety. There is no other way to substantiate or understand knowledge worthy of the name.

I would like to return to the four components of the ancient Greek idea of nature or concept of nature: the origin, goal, process and meaning of this process. This also touches on the question of man, indeed it is inseparable from it. Origin = arche, goal = telos. In this respect, we are arche-teleological beings. And that also means: time beings. We are what we were and what we will be. We are held in this timeless wholeness. It sustains us, guarantees us, allows us to grow towards the cosmic anthropos if we find our level of completion in it, i. e. that which can also be understood as Buddhahood.

People everywhere in the universe are struggling for high consciousness and fulfilment of being.

We are surrounded by roaring life. The lifelessness of modern cosmology is a delusion that is driving us all mad. It is strange that most people on this earth accept all this as if it could not be otherwise – to emphasise this once again.

The pathology of these ideas is palpable. The nocturnal firmament in its radiant majesty enables or at least induces a sense that life and intelligence exist everywhere, at least for a certain period of time, which is star related and variable.

What do the velvety splendour and the stars at its bottom conceal? Certainly not a meaningless wasteland; this dwells more in the brains of misguided earthlings. Why pull yourself up by the senseless, as many do, just because the cosmological models are the way they are, i. e. desolate constructs and hells?

You can see and interpret everything differently if you start from different premises. I have tried to show this again and again over the decades. It is other horizons of thought that I bring into play; these are certainly capable of acting as game changers, even if it doesn't look like it at the moment.

Finally, another encouraging word from Goethe:

"Is it such a great mystery what God, man and the world are? No! But nobody likes to hear it. So it remains a secret."

* * *

The Extraterrestrials

The question of extraterrestrial intelligent life is closely linked to the question of where these intelligences can develop, i. e. on which celestial bodies. And this brings us to cosmology, the study of the cosmos and the universe. From the point of view of modern cosmology, it is difficult, if not impossible, to determine the cosmic location from which these beings start, if they start from anywhere at all. That is not necessarily the case. But is this universally celebrated cosmology even true? There are well-founded doubts. At least I have held such doubts for more than fifty years. And I'm not the only one ...

Although mainstream cosmology is in a deep crisis – which most people are not even aware of – and from which it has not yet found its way out of, it is generally believed in as long as its basic assumptions are considered to be essentially correct. Those who don't are quickly marginalised. As is well known, there are plenty of cranks and fantasists ...

Who decides that, who determines that? And on the basis of what criteria? Who believes the cosmologists who set the tone almost everywhere and are on a first-name basis with the spirit of the world – that's as good as it gets? That is the question of the premises, the thinking and research presuppositions that are always involved, usually only implicitly. And the famous critical thinking, which is so ideologically popular, looks rather poor when it comes to cosmological questions – and that is what we are talking about here.

Even clever minds and intellectuals, who pride themselves

on their ability to scrutinise what is universally accepted, usually buckle here and capitulate to what physicists, astronomers and cosmologists carry around like a monstrance, knowing full well that the so-called laymen simply lack the criteria to judge this seriously and to distinguish between empiricism, hypotheses and pure fiction. You can't blame anyone for that. And yet, and yet, things are not quite that simple.

To a certain extent, we have to start from scratch with this topic, constantly ask ourselves new and fresh questions about the crucial issues that arise here, and not allow ourselves to be driven out of our own thinking by dogmas and authorities that are piling up threateningly everywhere. That's easy to say. But what does reality look like? Do we have more to offer than mathematised assumptions? What do we really know? Where are the solid foundations on which we can build our constructs of the world?

To begin with: How likely is it that we inhabitants of this small celestial body Earth have a unique status in the immeasurable depths and expanses of the universe, in the sense that there is and can be no one like us anywhere else? Put bluntly, this seems quite improbable.

Why should we be so extremely rare? There is actually nothing to suggest this. Nevertheless, assuming this ultimately leads to the bold hypothesis that the majority of the celestial bodies visible to us are not carriers of life and consciousness, but are merely decoration, as it were, an assembly of dead things that have nothing to do with anything.

The debate about whether or not there is extraterrestrial intelligent life is an old one: "Are we alone in space?" This is a question that has been asked again and again for decades. I myself have never asked this question because I have always assumed and still assume, and not just for reasons of probability, that we live in a world that is completely and utterly alive and that all hypotheses about our alleged rarity or – even more absurdly – uniqueness are ultimately based on false premises, on false assumptions and assertions that do not stand up to intelligent analysis.

The sea of galaxies that the mega-technical telescopes reveal to us is impressive, but without any deeper meaning. What do we see? This remains unclear and purely hypothetical. We don't even know what a galaxy really is, what stars really are, how they were formed and what is actually happening on them and with which actors. The well-known conclusions derived from observations using super telescopes are, seen in the light of day, nothing more than assertions. Everything can be explained completely differently. And anyway: everything is completely different from what it seems or appears.

What is presented as dead emptiness only reflects the dead emptiness of the viewer.

"The cosmos is like a mirror", goes an old Persian proverb. What we perceive in this mirror is ourselves. We judge the cosmic environment according to our own consciousness. All observations must be interpreted. They are not written in illuminated letters above the phenomena.

What is cosmic light? Perhaps primarily the result of space-energetic fields acting against each other, which are already alive per se, filled with bubbling life and consciousness. There is nothing dead and meaningless, instead, what we see everywhere are manifestations of the cosmic all-unity, of world space, which in its core substance is the world soul itself, as the cosmologist and philosopher Helmut Krause emphasises. We find similar statements as early as the great Renaissance philosopher Giordano Bruno.

The galaxies are not moving away from us, as the Big Bang fiction suggests, but are disappearing into the unfathomable expanse of living space because our cosmic organ of vision is weakening as part of an ageing process. The flight of the galaxies is based on an illusion. And so on.

Where can living and intelligent life unfold? As late as the 18th century, scholars were still of the opinion that all celestial bodies were alive and inhabited by rational beings. The philosopher Voltaire pondered whether the inhabitants of Sirius might not be far superior to the level of intelligence of the inhabitants of Earth. An interesting thought, after all, and one that can certainly be seriously considered. This thought may be wrong, but it is considerably more intelligent than the assertion that there is no life at all on Sirius.

In all my considerations, I myself always start from the living, not from the dead, from consciousness and not from beings blind to consciousness or things without a deeper meaning.

What do they look like, the so-called extraterrestrials, to pose this question once again? Probably quite similar to ourselves, so by no means monstrously different. Do they know about us, the super-smart earthlings who point their giant telescopes into the cosmic night in the strange hope of receiving signals that will give them information about the universe and the stars? Why would that be strange? Because I do not believe that it is possible to discover anything with these telescopes that is essential, that gives us real information about cosmic things in their substance and their vitality.

The earthlings use telescopes that are not intelligent per se or testify to intelligence. Ultimately, they only see themselves. The rest is a desolate desert. This is also their view of the world. "A gateway to a thousand deserts, silent and cold", as a Nietzsche poem puts it.

Many people think that when they think of extraterrestrial life, they are confronted with a civilisation that is far superior to earthly civilisation in terms of technology. This leads to the UFO topic, which has moved and worried people for decades and given rise to all kinds of speculation. I am rather unsure here. I don't know what the so-called UFOs actually are. I tend to think they are terrestrial objects, although I am well aware of the counter-arguments to this assumption.

And this also seems important to me: what does a high level of technical development say about the inhabitants of a star? Does it indicate something like cosmic intelligence? I don't think so. I would almost say just the opposite, although I have no final certainty here.

Cosmic intelligence, in the sense of spiritual-cosmic ability, is not linked to what is regarded here as high technical intelligence. These are different forms and degrees of consciousness. The highest forms and degrees of technical genius develop independently of the creative and, in this sense, spiritual-cosmic genius.

But I don't want to set up a dogma here that can't do justice to the complexity of these things. So I would like to leave it at these hints.

Observing the sky on a starry night evokes layers and depths in people that usually overwhelm them. Especially when it also awakens the cosmological claims in our consciousness that are presented everywhere as true and scientifically proven – which is by no means the case. The nocturnal firmament pulls us out of our earthly anchoring and confinement, so to speak. It expands and sublimates our consciousness, making it permeable and alive.

And we sense that we are not only the ones looking, but also the ones being looked at.

We stand in the open. Observed by the eternal cosmic eye, which we can never escape. In a sense, we ourselves become extraterrestrials, inhabitants of distant zones and horizons that seem strange and at the same time familiar and close. Distance becomes proximity. The here becomes there. We realise that we have always known ...

* * *

The Reanimation of the World

We are living through a global crisis of unimaginable proportions. The so-called corona crisis is only one part of this crisis, which can and must be described as a fundamental crisis of our entire being-in-the-world. This is because we are on the verge of destroying everything, physically, mentally and spiritually, that is part of the essence of our humanity on this planet. In this respect, the human being on earth is being put to the test. And things are not looking good, to put it mildly.

What is becoming brutally clear in the corona crisis has a long history, and in order to understand what is happening today, it is at first necessary to realise what abstract natural science, as it has been established since the 17th century, has to do with it and what characterises it at its core. Very few people realise this. This science has eliminated everything living from the outset or devalued it as "merely subjective".

This can be studied paradigmatically and as if in a burning glass with Galileo Galilei. The eminent historian of technology Lewis Mumford rightly refers to Galileo's "crime" in his book "The Myth of the Machine". I have been talking for decades about the blatant subject-blindness of the prevailing natural sciences. Even the much-vaunted quantum theory has not changed this, although the opposite is often claimed, as if it was the alternative program to mechanistic thinking. In fact, it is an extension of it, and as far as mathematisation is concerned, it is its crowning glory. Life remains as excluded as ever. Quantum theory cannot explain a blade of grass.

What counts as a scientific object for this science – and is treated in mathematical-analytical form – is precisely this: a mere thing that has no inside, i. e. no consciousness. Everything inside "natural things", when it emerges into independent ontological reality and effectiveness, is a disruptive factor that cannot be integrated into the cold grid view of the scientific mind, insofar as it is attached to the prevailing dogma of the outside world – and this is usually the case.

Only nature, imagined as a more or less dead outside world, can be quantified or mathematised, dissected and abstractly reassembled almost at will. This cannot be done with the living.

As it says in Faust (Mephistopheles, student scene):

"Whoever wants to recognise and describe
  something living,
  first seeks to drive out the spirit,
  then he has the parts in his hand,
  unfortunately! only the spiritual bond is missing."

This "spiritual bond" is only understood as an abstract one that has no dignity of its own. This is the brutal Procrustean bed that abstract natural science imposes on all of living nature and makes possible what has caused a furore in the form of a mega-technology today that has a grip on almost everything on this planet. In the long term, the abstract basic premise leads to the levelling of all living things, which has brought us to the brink of self-destruction.

I am talking about the Megatechnical Pharaoh, before whom the majority of earthlings lie prostrate. This glittering metallic idol whips the earthlings mercilessly forward, and they serve him predominantly with fervour. On the face of it, there is no need to exert any compulsion; they do their daily prostrations voluntarily. They have learnt to love the idol, they worship it and pay homage to it, and anyone who makes them dislike it is quickly punished and branded as an enemy of progress or science.

It is becoming increasingly clear where the journey is heading. Keyword: Great Reset. More on this later. At the same time, most earthlings have probably made themselves at home in a more or less dead, monstrous universe that they consider to be real, even though it grins at them with hostility, does not care about their weal and woe and, as I believe I have comprehensively demonstrated, is also only hypothetical, even fictitious, for long stretches. In this way, man on earth becomes a stranger, a cosmic outcast; one can also speak of a "cosmic idiot", as Peter Sloterdijk puts it. Not a flattering label.

Sloterdijk is referring to the irreversible basic condition of modern man as a cosmically lost being. Like many intellectuals, who are almost all believers in science, Sloterdijk considers a living cosmos that integrally includes man and assigns him his dignity to be obsolete or pure fantasy.

In my book "What the Earth Wants" from 1998, I spoke of a large-scale experiment in relation to humanity, which could be summarised in the question: "How many psychopaths does it take to ruin a star like the Earth?" Today, in the corona-virus crisis, this question is more relevant than ever.

Many people certainly think this is exaggerated, dismissing the whole issue in the belief – one could also say delusion – that the brilliant intelligence of the scientific, technical, digital and political elites will somehow sort it out for us all. After all, we have always managed to avert a total catastrophe so far. Why not now?

For me, the corona crisis was a kind of crash course on the human being as it has developed here for the most part, and also on what is so highly regarded as science, primarily meaning so-called abstract natural science, which is still the guiding principle of science today.

The corona crisis, as an integral part of the world crisis that we are currently experiencing, as noted above, was and is also a philosophical challenge for me. The fact that things have unfolded so massively and, in some ways, in such a nauseatingly dull and clumsy manner has astounded me.

The glistening, cold light reveals all the madness going on on this maltreated planet anyway, which actually could not really have been overlooked in the past.

But now, that is my impression, the hostile processes are simplifying, if you want to try calling it that. The ugly face of the technical idol, the Megatechnical Pharaoh, is glaringly visible with almost shocking clarity, regardless of all the utopias and promises of salvation that are supposed to conceal the whole thing.

Read the pamphlet on the "fourth industrial revolution" and also the one on the "Great Reset" by Klaus Schwab; in the latter, the co-author Thierry Malleret probably wrote the main part or at least set the basic tone. The ideal here is ob-viously the cyborg idiot deprived of his freedom and human dignity, who has small machines built into his body and somehow seems to enjoy it because he feels connected to the super intelligence of the technical homo deus, the god-like superhuman who guides us into the supernatural paradise that we can and will now create ourselves. "If there will be no God on earth, / we ourselves are gods" (22nd song of "Winterreise" by Wilhelm Müller and Franz Schubert).

I would like to interweave a thought here that many will reject. The technological mania is being driven forward by the servants of the Megatechnical Pharaoh, first and foremost by the so-called elites, who consider themselves intelligent and are admired by countless people. They set the course, in close contact with the powerful in politics, business and the financial industry. Together, they represent an enormous, globally active and almost unassailable power factor against which most people feel powerless and helpless.

As a result, they also shirk their responsibility to varying degrees, according to the motto: What can we do about it, since we are, so to speak, only recipients of orders or executors or players?

I don't think it's that simple: there are not just the few powerful perpetrators – the "bad guys" – on the one side and the many innocent victims on the other who "can't help it".

This also applies to the ecological crisis. The many "down there" are also actors, are co-players and, as such, also bear the responsibility that is inherent in the human condition. They, i. e. the many, cannot be completely exculpated.

Nevertheless, the people "up there" may not bear the sole responsibility, but they certainly bear the lion's share, especially as they comprehensively manipulate and control "the masses" and, depending on the situation, also exploit and mistreat them. The greater the power, the greater the responsibility and the resulting possibility – I will allow myself this fantasy – of having to answer to a "world tribunal" in the course of a global upheaval. Corona regimes all over the world are guilty and remain guilty. Like all other brutal and cruel regimes and apparatuses of power, including de facto fascism, which also comes in the form of eco-fascism and techno-fascism, as we can clearly see today.

I would like to interject here that the prevailing cosmology ultimately presents us with a kind of criminal universe, within which earthly fascism seems somehow provincial, if you consider the star-devouring super monsters of the so-called black holes, which are seriously believed to be real, although the projective part of them is actually palpable. A few years ago, a photo of such a black hole was even presented to an astonished world audience, which was applauded worldwide, but – after all – was then exposed by some, albeit very few, critical physicists, such as Alexander Unzicker, for what it is: a basically grotesque fake, a computer construct.

In the middle section of my video "What is cognition?" from August 2019, there is a commentary on this.

The fact that this catastrophic universe is the spawn of an essentially sick mind is something I have explained in detail in my book on cosmology "Räume, Dimensionen, Weltmodelle. Impulse für eine andere Naturwissenschaft (Spaces, dimensions, world models. Impulses for a different natural science)". If the world spirit has actually created such a world, it cannot be intelligent. I would then rather think of a malevolent Demiurgos, as imagined by the ancient Gnostics.

The abstract natural scientists and self-proclaimed cosmologists – who should rather be called chaologists – are in their own way the descendants of these ancient Gnostics.

The world formula mania that inspires many abstract minds is probably to be understood primarily in neo-gnostic terms. The dissolution or abstract vaporisation of the "real existing world" in the relevant formulary also means the annihilation of all living connections.

The world formula contains, or at least includes, world cancellation, as I showed many years ago. This is black alchemy of the worst kind. Another idol that many admire or worship. The matadors of transhumanism, who are increasingly gaining power and influence, also indulge in such idolatry. Strangely enough they do not or hardly recognise the precursors – and companions! – of their delusional ideas, i. e. the abstract natural sciences since Galileo.

The world crisis, including the corona crisis, is essentially a crisis of consciousness or, as I sometimes say, a psycho-cosmological crisis. The dominant formation of consciousness on this planet is that of intellectual culture.

Hardly anyone can escape this Moloch, especially as it is celebrated and offerings are constantly made to it. First and foremost in our way of life, and for me that always means cosmic-spiritual dignity. We lay this dignity at the feet of the mega-technical Imperator Mundi. He gladly accepts it. Why? Because he needs this living substance. If this substance is taken from him, all that remains is the dead and split-off technosphere, which cannot be saved from being dragged down into the Orcus that destroys all life on earth, even if it is upgraded to a theosphere.

The parasite needs the living host. If technical man, as a practising idolater, completely ruins the human, the spiritual-cosmic substance potentially inherent within him, he also destroys himself. And he knows or suspects this. The "steel skeleton" of global intellectual culture is dead and remains dead, and without the siphoning off and constant utilisation of that which constitutes man in his actual dignity, homo technicus is also at the end. He is dying of thirst in his abstract desert because he has filled up all living sources. And he will probably only realise this when it is too late. Technological imperialism disproves itself when it wins comprehensively, or when it thinks it has won. It implodes into its own nothingness ... It is clear that, like Hitler, it would involve as many people as possible in its downfall – I am deliberately using the subjunctive here.

I'll say it again because most people seem to ignore it – have I become a "preacher in the wilderness"? – : The prevailing abstract natural science, on which the whole edifice of our technical being-in-the-world is resting, is ultimately orientated towards a world devoid of people, a dead world, a world without life and consciousness.

A world without an inside, i. e. without consciousness, which only regards the outside as binding and is inhabited by a majority of beings who have forgotten or betrayed their actual inner being in the spiritual-cosmic sense, is not only absurd and inhuman, but also demonic. Whereby this demonisation must be continuously concealed, even denied, because otherwise the "acceptance of the crowd" is no longer given. Without the ongoing invocation of salvation, even redemption, through technological world domination, the Great Reset would not take effect.

In the end, it is about a kind of anti-life redemption that comes across as world salvation and world health. In the Corona madness, this is demonstrated in an almost woodcut-like manner.

The corona-virus regimes make use of such fantasies of saving the world, which always have a religious flavour, if they have not become a religion in the first place, and a dogmatic and totalitarian one at that.

I don't just mean the concept of demons in an intellectual-metaphorical way, to clear up any possible misunderstanding. There is evil, however we want to conceptualise it now. A discussion about the "ontology of evil", however, is largely pointless and only leads to that familiar form of ideological debate that produces nothing.

What is science anyway? The question is not easy to answer quickly. If you ask the scientists themselves, you will learn little of substance; the majority of them are blind to the foundations and prerequisites of their own work. In any case, the word "knowledge" is involved. Seen in the light of day, what is considered or claimed to be knowledge is often just a somehow plausible and consistent assertion about a phenomenon, a fact, a natural phenomenon, and so on.

Few things are truly self-evident and therefore a fact in the general consciousness, a fact that cannot be rationally and empirically questioned. The truth is not written in illuminated letters above the phenomenon to be interpreted or explained. The rational and-empirical approach is anchored in the intellectual culture, which first took shape around 2500 years ago in Greece and still determines what can and may claim validity as science today.

Science was initially and for a long time exclusively natural science, which developed out of natural philosophy and at some point began its triumphant march across the globe without it, indeed without epistemology and in-depth thinking at all. These are well-known facts – or at least they could be.

Less well known is the fact that science, or what is considered to be science, has never been and can never be detached from an overarching world view that encompasses and underpins the basic assumptions and premises without which science would be groundless in the first place. The premises are rarely mentioned directly and are often enough overlooked, but they are of essential importance.

For "world view", we can also say "ideology". This does not have to appear explicitly, but it does exist; it ultimately determines what is considered to be reality. Scientific controversies often arise from a different understanding of what is considered to be real. The famous controversy between Albert Einstein and Niels Bohr, the quantum theorists in general, is a paradigmatic example of this.

"Reality" is a difficult concept, often narrowed down to pure fact, the actuality of things or contexts. For all statements that go beyond direct sensory evidence, hypotheses come into play, which on closer inspection often turn out to be – partially useful – fictions. What is important here is the precision and predictive power conveyed by the mathematical description, of which physicists are particularly proud.

In a long conversation with Werner Heisenberg about fundamental questions of physics and Helmut Krause's field theory in the summer of 1974, I asked him to say in one sentence what his aim was as a physicist and scientist. His answer was: "I want to understand nature, and I want to understand it so precisely that predictions are possible." That is clear enough. Understanding is linked to – accurate – predictions. Is this a criterion for reality or even truth in scientific understanding? That depends on the premises that are set and that determine the cognitive process.

Anyone who represents a different basic assumption than that provided for in the prevailing intellectual culture and thus departs from the context of a different worldview, which I do, will interpret a phenomenon or natural thing differently than is accepted and honoured in the conventional framework. Predictions can still be made to a certain extent; they are just of a different kind or differently framed and are not, in the usual understanding of science, abstract and technically realisable.

People tend to consider something to be true or, more modestly, correct if it results in something "tangible" in the technical sense. Motto: My computer works, so the physical principles on which it is based have been perfectly proven. In short: What works is true.

Is that true? Not at all; but what works is at least technically correct in the first instance, from hoovers to smartphones, but it is precisely this functioning that often conceals what is missing and what represents the actual ontological and cosmic-natural basis. Example: What transports electromagnetic waves through space? The prevailing physics has no convincing answer to this question.

The famous ether theory, which moved and worried physicists in the 19th century, even overwhelmed them – they simply couldn't come to terms with it because this medium had to be incredibly dense and at the same time unimaginably fine and so on – was definitely more meaningful than the meaningless statement about the "quantum vacuum", which has no real explanatory value. I have dealt with these questions in detail in my cosmology book, also in my video about the Michelson-Morley experiment.
Modern science is inconceivable without its technical coun-

terpart. Most of today's astrophysical, cosmological or microbiological research would collapse immediately if the big plug was pulled, if it was disconnected from the abstract images and measuring instruments it needs to be fully convincing according to its own premises.

In this respect, science is an integral part of the technocratic dictatorship. And this in close connection with the centres of power and money. Genuine thinking plays a negligible role in science.

Philosophy is regarded there as a more or less beautiful intellectual game of glass beads that is "allowed to be", assuming, of course, that it does not make any overarching claims, especially those that question and challenge science in all its depth. The majority of scientists deny this challenge, even reject it indignantly. The actually interesting fundamental questions of natural philosophy fall by the wayside: What is light? What is gravity? Is it infinitely fast or does it have a measurable speed? Why does it penetrate everything? What holds the earth in space? Is this space a simple dead extension or a living, pulsating something to which the old term "world soul" could be applied – which is my assumption? And much more.

What about the technocratic dictatorship in the world crisis, which is increasingly taking our breath away and driving the more sensitive almost mad? Does philosophy have anything to say here or anything of substance to comment on? I would answer in the affirmative, but I am starting from an idea of philosophy that hardly anyone adheres to today. In the intellectual culture of the Megatechnical Pharaoh, the following applies: when science researches and speaks, the philosopher must remain silent, because – as is assumed –

what would he seriously have to say as long as he himself does not become a master of arithmetic, an abstract sorcerer's apprentice?

The high priests of the abstract do not want to be disturbed in their work, do not want to and cannot (!) ask the fundamental questions that are actually relevant, to emphasise this once again. That is why their view of the world is so bleak, so monotonous and monochrome; that is why it resembles more a nightmare, a delusion, a gigantic phantasmagoria.

This could be left alone if it did not reach deep into our core substance as living self-conscious human beings, self-conscious, with the result that it ruins us and destroys us mentally, stifling our creative imagination. And even further, what destroys the soul also destroys the living nature that sustains us. The mega-technical campaign of destruction that we are experiencing was prepared by a theoretical furore of destruction in our consciousness, which initially centred on ideology, on thinking that was becoming increasingly dead and detached.

But the real devastation follows close on the heels of the ideological devastation. Hiroshima is inconceivable without life-threatening physics. When Otto Hahn heard on the radio on 6 August 1945 in Farmhall in England, where he was interned with Werner Heisenberg, Max von Laue, Carl Friedrich von Weizsäcker and others, that the atomic bomb had been dropped on Hiroshima – Heisenberg initially doubted whether it really was one – he is reported to have said: "I have nothing to do with it." At the same time, everyone involved knew that his inner thoughts were completely different and that he was suicidal because he felt guilty. They were afraid for him.

Otto Hahn had once told Weizsäcker that he would kill himself if his discoveries resulted in an atomic bomb – albeit "in the hands of Hitler", as Weizsäcker said in an interview with "Der Spiegel" in 1967. Now it wasn't Hitler, it was the Americans. Nevertheless, it almost knocked him over.

These are processes that are part of the topic and need to be considered, although in later years physicists skilfully managed to shift the blame onto politicians and present themselves as "pure researchers". Robert Oppenheimer was more honest, at least for a brief moment, when he said in horror after the first atomic bomb was dropped in the Nevada desert on 16 July 1945: "We have done the devil's work."

Technology – on what scale? – has always had and continues to have an element of power that has dictatorial traits and presents itself as having no alternative. This element does not stop at the human core substance. This core substance is to be remodelled, "improved" and raised to a higher level.

The human being is to become a cyborg ghost, a robot without a self-determined ego and spirit: an externally determined hybrid being, as envisaged by the Great Reset, with technical implants in the body that become a part of this body that you can no longer get rid of, which is then always there and sings its satanic song: "You're protected, you're fine, you have everything you need, trust us, why do you have to torture yourself with questions and deeper thought processes, it's all going nowhere, we're building the better world for your benefit, for your joy and for global peace ..."
People are to become technical puppets. Why freedom, why

self-determination, why everything that used to burden people?

It is to be remodelled in such a way that it can be controlled without too much effort by the master race – not forgetting the ladies – of the digital corporations and the cathedrals of abstract power, which have already spiritually detached themselves from the living and are now in the process – it will take some time, just be patient – of eliminating this living in its entirety or almost in its entirety. Mentally and physically. This is pure nihilism, the "will to nothingness", as Nietzsche says. Perhaps someone still remembers the title of ecologist Herbert Gruhl's last book from 1992 "Himmelfahrt ins Nichts (Ascension into Nothingness)" with the subtitle "Der geplünderte Planet vor dem Ende (The plundered Planet before the End)"?

First of all, the matadors of abstract world domination are concerned with unbridled and transnational power, with the subjugation of humanity, and in order to enjoy this obscene amount of power, not everything must be destroyed, to mention this aspect once again. Some nature should and may be preserved. Later, at some point, perhaps faster than we think, the mind will mutate into a chip and AI (so-called artificial intelligence), and then it will go on, further and further, into the reconstruction and colonisation of the cosmic environment, as the quantum physicist Frank Tipler vividly described in 1994 in his monstrous book "Physics of Immortality" – technical salvation, technical immortality beckons.

The book became a mega bestseller for months! The esotericists were thrilled. In this delusional idea, the imperfect, biologically carnal human being mutates into a perfect simulation of himself – he doesn't even realise the difference –

and is then indestructible, immortal. Blessed in madness, blessed in delusion, an eternal ghost ... Religious delusion in the guise of abstract natural science.

The plan of creation is "repurposed", to use a term coined by the '68ers, into a technical plan designed by the sorcerer's apprentices. Goethe depicted the basic pattern of this madness in his poem "The Sorcerer's Apprentice", which is of oppressive topicality. The sorcerer's apprentices, all of them, will fail when "sacred nature" (Friedrich Hölderlin) awakens to itself and the great separation of spirits rises like a radiant star, driving away the ghosts and banishing them to where they strive and from where they come. I allow myself this little poetic, but not only poetic, reverie, which revitalises me again and again and gives me confidence when the madness that rages here and will not go away and is flooding me.

This leads to the question of a saving, in some sense promising perspective. Without this perspective, we remain blocked and powerless, but where should we look for it and, if necessary, find it? Where is the trail that is worth following? As far as the eye can see, nothing of the sort can be recognised.

What one perceives predominantly resembles the desolate land of the Grail tale. And there is little hope. And yet there is this trace. I am convinced of that. I don't believe in the destruction of the earth. The creative will prevail.

The familiar objection rings in my ears: "But dear Mr Kirchhoff! What is that? Do you seriously believe that? It's fatally reminiscent of Martin Heidegger's infamous statement in the interview in "Der Spiegel" from 1966: 'Only a God can save us'. Is that what you mean? Isn't that wishful thinking or, worse still, some kind of esoteric phant-asmagoria?"

We don't get any further with Heidegger, although the sentence, taken by itself, doesn't have to be wrong. Everything here depends on what is meant by "a god" – why not also "a goddess". It cannot be something religious, as it is commonly understood. Fine, but what then? I will try to at least hint at where I see a saving impulse. And to do that, I need to expand a little. First of all, a few encouraging lines from Goethe:

"Despite all forces,
  keeping yourself,
  never bowing down,
  showing strength.
  Thus call upon the arms of the gods."

Instead of "a god" now "the arms of the gods".

Are they higher beings than guardians and custodians of the earth? Yes, that definitely resonates. Like Goethe himself, I want to leave that up in the air for now.

What does rescue mean? Salvation from what and salvation for what? It is the same as with freedom; here, too, we can ask what from and what for. Salvation has to do with this "keeping oneself". This concerns the individual and, naturally, the heavenly body that nourishes and sustains him, which is not an oasis in the midst of a cosmic desert, but can be understood as embedded in the all-aliveness of the universe, or perhaps more modestly: in the currents and vibrations of our cosmic environment or "neighbourhood" that surround and permeate us. "Space is world soul", says the philosopher and cosmologist Helmut Friedrich Krause (1904 to 1973).

That convinces me. The outside-only space is a fiction. It doesn't exist, it can't exist. This can be derived purely phenomenologically from our directly experienced physicality. We do not live and breathe in the ultimately abstract "local space" (Hermann Schmitz), as described by mathematics and physics, but in an all-round living and consciousness-filled medium that completely eludes scientific grid searches.

Incidentally, and as it were a comment in passing: the question of space has never been solved scientifically and intellectually; it remains a great mystery. No physicist or mathematician really knows what space is, any more than they know what light is, what gravity is, what consciousness is, what the stars are and what life is and how it came into being. Only from a cosmology of all-aliveness can we seriously approach the question of whether there can be something like salvation and healing, initially against all evidence of mercilessly advancing destruction.

The earth is a living organism, and so are the other stars. I am convinced that super-hot spheres or thermonuclear hells – as the stars are seen by the prevailing astrophysics and astronomy – falling around each other in icy night and eternal senselessness, do not exist. Here I am drawing on Helmut Krause's thoughts, which I have tried to take further. What appears to us as cosmic light is the result of subtle and very differentiated interactions of the space energy radiations of the stars surrounding us, above all the sun, which is not a hellish star, but an all-round living sphere, like all so-called suns.

A gaseous, billowing star of such immense heat, as is assumed – it has never been definitively proven – is a physical monster that could never function and appear as a clearly defined sphere. What we see is a circular disc with a clearly recognisable boundary which, in relation to the whole celestial body, indicates a solid rather than a gaseous structure below the surface layer.

The astrophysical assertions about the physics of the sun and cosmic light are fictions, arising from arithmetic operations and extrapolations based on the physics of the earth's surface as we know it. This is methodical geocentrism (short formula: "Everything as it is here"), in which interacting spatial energy fields have no place. The maths provided here would only have probative value if these fields did not exist. I have commented on this in detail elsewhere, most extensively in the aforementioned book "Räume, Dimensionen, Weltmodelle. Impulse für eine andere Naturwissenschaft (Spaces, dimensions, world models. Impulses for a different natural science)", but also in several videos.

The Earth ("Gaia") as part of the all-round living and consciousness-filled galaxy – there are countless living and inhabited stars in it – will, like every organism, try everything to "preserve itself", to muster its own organic as well as mental and spiritual immune system in order to ward off the threatening destructive energies. People who really become aware of their innermost nature as cosmic-spiritual beings contribute to this. I am putting this forward here without further substantiation as a thesis and thought meditation.

"Thoughts are effective factors of the universe", says Novalis. Apparently there is a ghostly struggle in the cosmos, an antagonism of creative and destructive, regressive forces.

Numerous myths and mythologems as well as neo-myths in books and films tell of this, and philosophers such as Heraclitus, Giordano Bruno, Jakob Böhme, Friedrich Wilhelm Joseph Schelling, Friedrich Nietzsche – with some exceptions –, Helmut Krause and Jochen Kirchhoff also do it in their own way. We are involved in this spirit wrestling, whether we like it or not. And in the case of the earth, this spirit wrestling is particularly difficult for the creative spirits.

The demonic forces have already gained a threatening amount of ground here and are defending their bastions with all the finesse and brutality at their disposal. We have not yet succeeded in checkmating them, in rendering them harmless. But succeed we will. It will succeed if it is possible in principle. What is possible here will happen. That is my assumption. And it will certainly require a certain kairos, a certain higher constellation that cannot be tapped into in advance. This kairos and this spirit wrestling are not fantasy, dear readers. Many of you already suspect that something like this is happening, if my perception is not mistaken.

There are plenty of transitional and end-time scenarios. In the film "The Matrix", especially in the first part, the future is obviously foreshadowed or hinted at, however this will play out in reality. Ultimately, the film is about waking up to reality. This awakening is difficult, very difficult. But the world crisis could make it easier. No one is standing on neutral ground, so to speak. Everyone has to – at some point – show their colours. And formulaically, I would say:

Get out of the matrix of annihilation and gagging and wake up! From "cosmic idiot" to "cosmic anthropos". Perhaps it is appropriate to speak of a metaphysical revolution.

This includes countless concrete decisions and steps on the part of the creative spirits. Everything will depend on who we really are when "it counts". And that doesn't just mean the implied kairos at some point in the near or distant future, but the here and now. Now is what matters. The servants of the Megatechnical Pharaoh are not tired, but full of frightening vigour. But we should not overestimate our opponent, and of course we should not underestimate him either.

The idols have already been "eaten away", their servants are lashing out because they sense the threat. In this respect, this current phase is particularly dangerous, but also hopeful.

In one of his writings (from 1584), the great thinker Giordano Bruno summed it up in a succinct formula that reveals a militant and programmatic impetus: "Lo spaccio della bestia trionfante", or "The expulsion of the triumphant beast". This is what it should and will be about now and in the future.

* * *

Sources

Manova Magazin
manova.news

The Corona Blues
    Der Corona-Blues (25.04.2023)

Torn between East and West
    Zerrissen zwischen Ost und West (17.09.2024)

The Return of Life
    Die Rückkehr des Lebens   (21.04.2022)

The Fullness of Light of the Living
    Lichtfülle des Lebendigen (26.08.2022)

The Melancholy of the Nearness to Death
    Die Wehmut der Todesnähe (29.10.2022)

An Epochal Winter Journey
    Eine epochale Winterreise (08.12.2022)

The Newfound Splendour of Things
    Der neu gefundene Glanz der Dinge (19.10.2023)

The World Without Us
    Die Welt ohne uns (17.08.2023)

The Extraterrestrials
    Die Extraterrestrischen   (29.02.2024)

The Reanimation of the World
    Die Wiederbeseelung der Welt I   (19.02.2022)
    Die Wiederbeseelung der Welt II   (24.02.2022)

Institut für kritische Gesellschaftsforschung
kritischegesellschaftsforschung.de

Realisation and Delusion. The Problem of
Science in the World Crisis
    Erkenntnis und Wahn. Das Problem der Wissenschaft
    in der Weltkrise   (Januar 2022)

Cicero Online – Magazin für politische Kultur
cicero.de

The Devil's Labourers
    Die Arbeiter des Teufels   (02.08.2023)

About the Author

Jochen Kirchhoff, born in 1944, lives and works in Berlin. He gave around 150 lectures on natural philosophy topics in the 1990s and early 2000s, some of which are reproduced here as transcripts. So far, only some of the lectures have been published as podcasts and transcripts. He has also given over 400 public lectures on natural philo-  sophy and socially relevant topics since 1980. Numerous seminars on geomantic topics and the holistic reception of classical music, among others, round off his teaching activities. He has also published philosophical talks on his YouTube channel, which also address contemporary phenomena from a philosophical perspective. His literary work to date includes his tetralogy of natural philosophy, works on the philosophy of music, monographs, contributions to journals and writings on the preservation, reappraisal and creative cultivation of Helmut Friedrich Krause's philosophical work. Jochen Kirchhoff is a recognised expert on the work of Giordano Bruno, Friedrich Wilhelm Schelling, Novalis, Friedrich Nietzsche, Arthur Schopenhauer and Helmut Friedrich Krause, among many others. He regularly contributes essays and interviews to the social discourse on contemporary phenomena and fundamental questions on overcoming the crisis of human consciousness from a philosophical perspective.

jochenkirchhoff.de